Always

Hope

What people are saying about The Watchers by Deirdra Eden

"This story will fire young readers' imaginations and
keep them turning every page to the thrilling end."
~ Joyce DiPastena, RWA Heart of the West winning
author of *Loyalty's Web* and *Illuminations of the Heart*

"Deirdra is a passionate and insightful storyteller."
~ Stephanie Abney, *Deseret News*

"Deirdra Eden writes with passion and purpose . . .
Knight of Light is destined to become a fan favorite!"
~ Michele Ashman Bell, *Meridian Magazine* and
author of the *Butterfly Box Series*

"This is one of the greatest fairy tales ever told. Knight of Light
is more than just a book, it is a epic allegory comparable
to the works of C.S. Lewis and other great Christian writers."
~ Penny A. Reay, Talent Managemet President of
HKT Productions

THE WATCHERS

KNIGHT OF LIGHT

DEIRDRA EDEN

Eden Literary, LLC

Knight of Light
By
Deirdra Eden
Book 1 of The Watchers Series

Cover Design by Eden Literary, LLC
Book Layout by Keani Gifford

Special graphics AKaiser/Shutterstock.com
Image copyright tanatat/Shutterstock.com and Vangelis76/Shutterstock.com

ISBN: 978-0-9960158-0-6
Also Available in eBook Format

For a Free Copy of The Watchers Coloring Book, visit
https://www.smashwords.com/books/view/429719
and enter coupon code AZ54J

Knight of Light / Deirdra Eden
2nd Edition, January 2015
Text type was set in Garamond

THE WATCHERS SERIES

Dedicated To:

The Master Storyteller
The one who shapes all our stories into a work of art.

Acknowledgments

I started writing this book when I was fifteen, but didn't get it published until in my thirties. It's been a long epic journey that has built my character as I have built the characters. Many of the people and events in The Watchers Series are based on real people and events that have come into my life. I've obviously changed the names to protect identity and used many symbolisms so you don't feel as you are reading a fifteen-year-old's journal.

During the last decade, there have been many good people who have encouraged and inspired me. My dad has been awesome through this whole processes and has read every messed up manuscript I pushed toward him. Thanks, Dad!

There have been at least 70-100 authors in ANWA and other writers' groups that have read the manuscript, torn it apart, and made me put it back together. I refined my skills, characters and flushed out things that weren't really important.

On my computer, I have over a hundred different versions of the manuscript that I worked on as my own personal life has been torn apart and put back together. This was part of my personal story as my character was being built. I edited out things that weren't really important, refined my skills, faced demons, found epic friends, and learned what God's title of "Author and Finisher" really means.

It would be impossible for me to acknowledge everyone who has helped me over the last decade. I'd be sure to forget someone. There have been many great authors and editors who have read it. Know that I am thanking you now. Thank you for pointing me in the right direction and cheering me on when I needed it most. Thank you also to my team of editors, promotion specialists and friends who helped me make it through this last long haul to finally see this book in print.

~ Contents ~

Chapter One

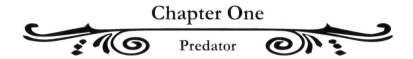

Predator

England - 1270 A.D.

Flames spewed in waves of red heat from the windows. Hot ash floated into the sky like smoldering snow. Screams from the children inside the burning cottage pierced the darkness.

"We've got to help them!" I shouted and covered my ears to muffle the agonizing pleas of the trapped children. Surfacing memories haunted me of the fire that killed my parents three years earlier.

"Let the men handle this, Auriella. Death isn't something a young lass should see." The village elder leaned heavily against his walking stick. His statement was false comfort. I had already seen death and never wanted to again.

The fire ravaged the straw rooftop. Able-bodied adults raced to and from the brook with buckets of water.

The elder shook his head in frustration. "If it weren't for me bad leg I'd be able to help."

I had two perfectly good legs. I was only thirteen, but I was fast and

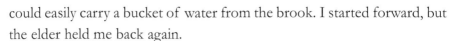

could easily carry a bucket of water from the brook. I started forward, but the elder held me back again.

"These fires aren't normal. They start too fast," the elder grumbled. "If you ask me, with how frequent and spread out these attacks have been, it's got to be many arsonists working together."

Staring at the bright flames, the illusion of security I had created for myself evaporated. A horrifying thought suddenly struck me.

"What if it's the Shadow Legion causing these fires?" I asked.

"Nonsense!" the village elder almost shouted. "The Shadow Legion only kills important people like kings and nobles. They'd never come to our tiny village when London is less than a league away. It's definitely arson. The men at the tavern say several peasant homes with young girls have been targeted." He looked down at me with wary eyes. "Girls with flaming red hair like yours." He swallowed hard, making his Adam's apple bob. I swallowed too and looked back to the fire.

The elder cleared his throat. "No, it has to be arsonist. The Dark Legion is not that selective. Besides, if we are ever invaded by the Shadow Legion, the Lady of Neviah and the Immortal Watchers will save us."

I could not argue. All the stories I had heard coincided with what he was saying. No one knew where the Shadow Legion came from, but they were unrelenting lords of chaos. The inhuman legionnaires were unstoppable ravagers of death. Their nightmarish ranks consisted of ghostly wraiths whose whispers could poison the minds of even the purest of men.

No mortal stood against the Shadow Legion and lived. That was why the Lady of Neviah and the immortal protectors, the Watchers, were sent to live among us.

The children coughed and screamed for help from inside the cottage.

I wrung my apron in my hands. It was happening just like last time—flames, smoke, terror . . . the agonized screams. It would end in death just as before.

A toddler's silhouette flashed across the window. A few villagers still frantically threw buckets of water onto the house. Nearly the entire village stood before it, mouths agape, eyes wide in hopeless terror.

The Lady of Neviah wasn't coming tonight and someone had to save those children. Before my mind knew what my body was doing, I jumped forward into the burning cottage and bounded over the scorching rubble into the inferno.

I had just thrown myself into my nightmares. I was frightened, but it was too late to change my mind now. The wave of heat hit me like a wall of boiling water. I braced myself and stepped over a smoldering support beam. My skirt brushed against it and burst into a sheet of flames. I spun the cloth in my fists and quickly smothered the fire.

Three children huddled together in the corner.

I grabbed the toddler and shouted above the roaring flames and snapping wood, "Hurry, stay close behind me!

Small hands gripped what was left of my skirt. My bare feet sunk into the hot ash. The smoldering cinders felt no warmer than golden sand on a sunny beach as I held the children close and navigated through the collapsing cottage.

A blazing heap of rubble stood between us and the door.

"We can't get over!" the eldest child shouted and pointed to the debris blocking our way out.

Stones from the chimney crumbled to the floor. The roof bowed, threatening to give way on us.

I boosted the children, one at a time, over the burning debris and out the door. I clenched my teeth and put my hand against the scorching beam to support myself. My fingers tingled against the wood that pulsed with hot embers. I could taste the ash as I inhaled it. My lungs felt dryer with each breath I took.

Before I could leap to safety, the last support beam snapped. Rubble collapsed on me like raining brimstone and slammed me to the ground. My hand sank into the embers as I struggled to push myself up from the red-hot inferno. Sweltering shards of wood rolled down my hair and into my face.

Squinting against the hail of sparks, I shimmied between two fiery beams and onto the wet grass outside the cottage.

I lay on my back and took in a breath of fresh, cool night air. Blue and white stars sparkled overhead, contrasting the orange glow and heat of the cottage. I did it. The children were safe.

"Is she alive?" someone asked.

I took several more breaths, just to make sure I truly was alive before I whispered, "Yes, I'm alive." My mind raced over what had just happened. I imagined the burns which surely riddled my body. Oddly, I couldn't remember ever getting burned before, not from the boiling hot cauldrons I'd labored over and stirred to earn my keep, nor even from the fire that had taken my parents. I'd heard that being burned alive was one of the most painful ways to die. Knowing that my parents had died that way added to the agony I felt after I was orphaned.

I rolled onto my side. Nothing hurt yet, so I pushed myself up.

The three young girls were with their parents, who kissed their ash-covered faces and blonde heads.

I looked at my ravaged clothes and suppressed a groan. The tie of my apron hung against the shreds of my charred skirt. The fire had consumed

one full sleeve of my blouse, but my skin still glowed like pure ivory. It would take weeks to earn enough to replace my clothes.

"Thank you," the children's mother said, squeezing me to her chest as she cried.

"You shouldn't be thanking her," a man's cold voice called from the crowd.

The bystanders parted a path and bowed to the nobleman as he advanced toward me. The lord's dark cloak and polished black boots contrasted with the silver sword glinting at his side. His features were sharp and pointed, his eyes narrowed with distaste. I flinched as he pinched one of my red locks between his fingers and let it fall back over my shoulder.

He turned to the gathering crowd. "Not even a hair on her head was singed. Tell me, how does a girl manage such a feat?"

No one answered. A few people shifted their weight and wrung their hands together. The children's clothes, like mine, were in tatters, but angry burns covered their exposed skin and feet like cankers.

The nobleman leaned so close I could smell his sulfuric breath. His pupils narrowed to a slit as he focused on me. "I know who you are," he hissed, sounding more serpentine than human.

Who did he think I was? I stumbled away from him, walking backward until my back pressed against a nearby cart. The corner of his lips turned up in a dark smile, and his snake-like eyes went wild with hunger.

He turned to the crowd. "I tell you, she's a witch."

"No!" I shouted. "I'm not a witch."

"A witch!" someone called out.

Another bellowed, "That explains why she was the only survivor when her parents died."

"She has to be some kind of demon," a woman added. "Look at her

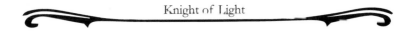

skin. It's not even flushed."

The nobleman lunged at me, seizing my wrists before I could move.

"I'm not a witch." I defended and tried to pull away.

"You have condemned yourself by speaking. All witches say those exact words." The nobleman squeezed my wrists tighter until I writhed in pain under the crushing pressure.

"Are you sure she's a witch?" someone asked. "She just saved three children."

"I'll prove it." The nobleman dragged me back to the smoldering cottage.

I fought uselessly to pry his fingers from my arms.

"Let go of me," I demanded. "I'm human."

The nobleman leaned forward and whispered just loud enough for me to hear, "You're no more human than I am, but you're not a witch either. You, my lady, are something much more powerful."

He lifted my hands to his face and inhaled the scent of my wrists. His eyes glazed over, and he shivered sinisterly.

I struggled frantically, unable to break away from his grasp. "You! You're a Shadow Lord!" I tried to scream, but it came out as a quiet gasp.

The creature pushed me closer to the fire and tried to force my hand onto a hot metal nail. "Go ahead, say it louder. No one is going to believe a young orphan girl. You are worthless to them. They will execute you as a witch and your blood will be mine."

Fear surged through my body and the instinct for survival took over. I kicked up the burning rubble at my feet and showered him with hot embers. He released his grip just long enough for me to twist free. I raced toward the edge of the village, sprinting over sharp rocks and twigs, ignoring the pain on my bare feet.

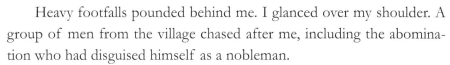

Heavy footfalls pounded behind me. I glanced over my shoulder. A group of men from the village chased after me, including the abomination who had disguised himself as a nobleman.

I turned toward the haunting Forbidden Forest. Images of every forest monster and demon from the villagers' stories flashed through my mind. I clenched my fists and forced myself to see past the hot, blinding tears brimming my eyes. I had no choice but to hide in the woods. They wouldn't follow me there . . . at least, the humans wouldn't. I prayed I would find a place to hide from the Shadow Lord as well.

Like a stag fleeing a predator, I raced into the forest and darted between trees and rocks. The wiry forest clawed at my skin and ragged clothes, forcing me to slow as I snapped the branches to free myself. I held out my arms to navigate the dark unfamiliar woods. Not even the light of the moon shone through the thick canopy of darkness.

I stopped and listened. The wind howled through the treetops like a starving wolf, but there was no sound from my pursuers. I slowed my pace and wandered deeper into the Forbidden Forest.

People thought the Shadow Legion lived in these dark woods. I wrapped my arms around my waist and shivered. I trudged forward into the darkness. I had no doubt the nobleman was actually part of the Shadow Legion. I would never forget the foul stench of his breath, his snake-like eyes, and menacing voice.

I walked until morning light filtered through the leafy canopy in bright patches and tingled my skin with a mixture of sun and shade. Exhausted, I leaned against a mossy oak and let my fingers sink into the tender moist bark. I knew I could never go back to my village.

I clenched the edge of my fire-ravaged dress. No one would employ me in this condition. Work for an orphan like me was hard to come by,

and looking like a desperate vagabond would make it infinitely worse.

After my parents' death, I traveled from home to home, cleaning and cooking, where I could. In return, I was paid meagerly.

My village took pity on me because my parents had lived there and had been respectable, although poor. Any other place I went would not be so welcoming. Some places ran beggars out of town or even stoned them, fearing them as thieves.

The wind danced through my hair, tossing my locks like scarlet streamers in a windstorm. A bird chirped a cheery melody, breaking the sound of silence. I paused from my thoughts and focused on the sounds of the forest. The trickling sound of water running over stones came from a clearing.

I made my way to the edge of the clearing by the stream. The tall grass waved around me like sheets of emerald silk. I noticed a shepherd standing in the center of the meadow, watching a small flock of sheep.

I ducked low in the grass.

The shepherd scanned the woods with a wary eye. People traded news on the main roads, and the whole countryside was probably looking for me by now. Everyone thought I was a witch.

I crawled through the foliage toward a willow tree and pulled back the vines like a curtain. I sat in the grotto of twisted roots dipping into the stream and put my lips to the water. I drank and wiped my mouth on my only remaining sleeve. I sat against the tree and pulled my knees to my chest.

I still couldn't believe it. How could they accuse me of being a witch? That place had been my home my entire life. The villagers knew my parents before they died. I was not evil.

I wiped my eyes with my fingertips, then cupped a handful of water

from the stream and bathed my dirty feet. The water momentarily stung the cuts as I washed out the dirt.

A branch snapped behind me. I whirled around. My eyes darted toward the dense woods. The trees stood still as if holding their breath. Opaque clouds moved across the sun, and the world dimmed around me. The air grew icy cold. My warm breath hit the frigid air and rose from my lips like white fog. Something was wrong.

I stood and peered out of my fortress of foliage. Black smoke billowed through the woods, enveloping everything in mists of darkness.

Fear paralyzed my body, and my heart sprinted.

"Wolves, wolves!" the shepherd cried out.

Wolves descended from the woods and flooded the meadow. Their matted fur stuck out in every direction like black spikes.

A wolf lunged for the sheepdog and viciously shook it. It was then I realized how big the black wolves really were. They were the size of oxen, but moved with swift predatory hunger. The sheepdog struggled to free itself from the massive jaws of the black wolf.

The savage pack tore into the flock, their fangs sliced through white wool, now splattered in red blood. Lamb carcasses lay strewn about the ground. The wolves were not there to eat, but to kill.

I huddled close to the tree. I closed my eyes, but couldn't shut out the horrible mix of howling wolves and bleating sheep.

Hot breath washed over my neck. My eyes sprang open. I whirled around.

Black flames billowed off the alpha wolf, and its savage eyes flashed like crimson brimstone. The beast snarled, unveiling lethal teeth.

The image of the sheepdog struggling in a piercing grip flashed across my mind. I fell back and slid away.

"Don't try to run," the Shadow Wolf spoke in a deep, masculine voice. "We know who you are."

"What?" I asked, dumbfounded that the beast was speaking to me. How many more nightmares would spring to life today? I tried to scream, but mists of darkness caught in my throat and suffocated my cry.

"That's right," the wolf growled. "You have no idea how many centuries we've waited for you." He lunged toward me.

I threw my arms over my head and slammed the heel of my foot into the snapping muzzle. The wolf latched onto my leg and shook. My flesh ripped opened in jagged tears. Adrenalin and heat rushed through my veins. My body pulsed with pain and the thumping of my heart pounded in my ears. I shrieked and tried to pull my mangled leg from the powerful jaw. He yanked back and buried his teeth deeper into my skin.

My fingers strained and sank into the earth. The Shadow Wolf dragged me back into the Forbidden Forest. My hands smoldered with heat and streams of smoke rose from my fingertips as I clawed at the ground.

Chapter Two

Sisters of Power

My face pressed against the cold dirt floor of an unfamiliar, dim room. I took a breath of dusty air, laced with the thick scent of rotting wood and mold. I coughed out the bitter taste of decay. Pain shot through my bones like hot metal. I strained for my mangled leg, but leather straps held my wrists together. Dark blood spotted the filthy bandages lining my calf.

I held my breath. My eyes darted around the room. Where was the wolf? Why hadn't I been killed? Why were my hands bound? Who would hold an injured girl captive?

Rows of dusty, knotted pine shelves held jugs and glass bottles of all sizes. Gnarled roots dangled from cracks in the ceiling. I writhed, struggling to free my hands until the straps cut into my wrists. A fireplace smoldered with amber and crimson coals pulsing through the ash. The only sunlight came from a tiny, dim window full of cobwebs.

"This is not a good place to be," I whispered to myself. I put the

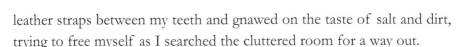

leather straps between my teeth and gnawed on the taste of salt and dirt, trying to free myself as I searched the cluttered room for a way out.

I saw two doorways. The first was dark, as if leading to some abyss, but bright sunlight beamed like a halo between the edges of the other door.

I opened my mouth and dabbed the bad taste of old leather on the sleeve of my dress. I could get the straps off later, but first I needed to get far away from this place.

I pushed myself off the floor to stand. Pain shot through my bandaged leg and gripped my stomach with pure agony, threatening to make me vomit. I fell back and sank into a beast of shadowy fur and powerful muscles.

Red eyes and wicked teeth contrasted with the long, black snout and matted fur of the Shadow Wolf. I shrieked, causing the spiders in the window to flee to the corner.

I jolted away from the wolf and scurried across the dirt floor on my forearms. My injured leg dragged behind me like dead weight. The wounds reopened and fresh blood soaked through the bandages. I knew I was going to be eaten this time.

I lifted my bound hands over my head and braced myself for another attack. When nothing happened, I took several short breaths and opened one eye.

The wolf's tongue hung lifeless from a gaping jaw of blood-stained teeth. I had no doubt the blood was mine.

The dark wooden door in the back of the cottage screeched open on broken hinges. A shriveled old woman rushed toward me with an erratic stride. "Yer awake! What be yer name?" The hag seemed excited and paid no attention to the massive wolf lying in a crushed heap on the floor.

I pointed at the evil beast. I couldn't catch my breath to press out audible words.

With one hand, the old woman grasped the massive wolf and shook it like an old coat. "Yes, it be dead. It tried ta kill ye, it did. But I, Hazella Lamia, saved ye."

The wolf's corpse was bigger than Hazella, but the old woman held it like it was weightless. "I sees this old wolf tryin' ta eat ye in the woods. I crushed its skull in, I did." Hazella gripped the wolf's leg and snapped it back to prove her point.

Hazella smiled, showing a mouth of jagged teeth. She pressed the wolf's body against the table and swung a knife into it. "Now we be eatin' it," Hazella cackled. A crazed look danced in the old hag's colorless eyes as she ripped the flesh from the wolf and tossed it into the pot over the fire.

"Be ye hungry?" Hazella asked in a tactless, cheery tone. I covered my nose to muffle the smell of Hazella's rancid clothing covered in blood and sewage.

I had to find a way to escape. I glanced at the door leading outside. Maybe I could fight through the pain of my mangled leg and run.

The old woman twisted her lips and squinted. "I don't needs no troublemakers or liars. I know yer hungry. See this here necklace?" With the bloody knife, Hazella tapped a brilliant ruby necklace hanging over her sagging bosom. "This here necklace is gettin' old, and I needs ta make a new one. The problem be those pixies. Until I gets a new one, I needs yer help. Once I gets it, then I will leave ye where I found ye, if yer a good girl." The last words trailed from her lips like a threat.

I couldn't imagine how I could help the old woman. The hag was so strong, while I couldn't even walk.

Hazella hobbled toward the sooty pot, filled a bowl with steaming

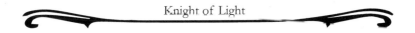

wolf stew, then dropped it in front of me. "Eat. It'll help ye ta feel better, or I'll give ye ta the wolves now."

I couldn't fight off the old woman. Hazella could snap a bone in two like a piece of dry straw. I had to come up with some kind of escape plan.

Hazella swung her knife toward me. The knife whistled through the air and slit the leather straps between my wrists. I jumped and slid back. The hag held the knife ready at her side and eyed me in the same inhuman way the Shadow Wolf had. "What be yer name, girl?"

I rubbed my raw wrists. "I'm no one, just a servant." I wasn't about to give a crazy woman my real name. "Everyone just calls me girl," I answered.

Hazella put her hands on her hips and leaned forward. "I'm just a servant too, and I wants to know why this here Shadow Wolf was takin' ye ta Lord Erebus." Hazella pointed to the lifeless wolf lying skewered across the table. Its bowels spilt like red noodles to the floor.

My jaw dropped. I couldn't think of any reason why Lord Erebus, leader of the Shadow Legion, would want me. I shook my head. "I don't know," I answered.

Hazella tilted her head and eyed me with one bulging eye as if trying to look into my soul. "Very well, girl. Ye must be my servant now and never try ta leave nor go beyond sight of this here cottage, or the hungry wolves will eat ye." Hazella plopped into a chair next to the fire and sipped on her Shadow Wolf stew. "We be sisters you and I," Hazella muttered casually.

I stared at the wolf stew in front of me and pretended to be interested in eating it. Hazella was the oldest person I had ever seen before. How could the crazy witch think we were sisters?

"Yes," Hazella hissed. Her gnarled fingers strained like claws around her bowl. "Sisters of power. We 'ave more in common then ye know."

Chapter Three

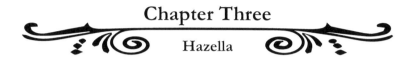

Hazella

Autumn leaves crunched under my bare feet. Despite the hideous scar on my calf, my leg had healed well since the wolf attack last spring.

Yet, even though the wound looked better, I flexed my feet back and stretched the repairing tendons and muscles each night. I still walked with a marked limp, but soon I would be able to run again.

I swung an empty bucket in my hand and enjoyed the crisp air as I walked to the stream. Like magic, the summer had changed to autumn; and, despite my situation, I sensed a magical change was about to happen in my own life as well. My heart burned in anticipation.

"Hurry up, girl!" Hazella screeched from the cottage doorway.

I quickened my pace and dropped the empty bucket into the stream. My leg should be strong enough by winter to run away, but the wolves were always hungry and the most aggressive during the winter. That meant I would have to wait until next spring.

"Ye better hurry," Hazella yelled again. "Them wolves eat bad

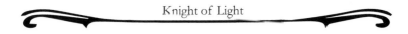

children who wander too far from home."

I wanted to be cheeky and say, "Then it's a good thing I'm not a child," but I wouldn't let myself take a chance of standing up to her. I had to keep pretending to be the victim. The old woman had the strength of an army and the mind of a lunatic. Catching Hazella off guard was the only way I could escape.

I seized the pail from the stream and hobbled dramatically so Hazella wouldn't know how well I was healing. Water sloshed in my bucket, but I tried my best not to spill. I knew if I lost even a drop, Hazella would shriek like a banshee until noon.

Hazella's dugout cottage blended in with the forested landscape. Only the smoky stone chimney made its own statement—sticking prominently out of the knoll. Grasses and wildflowers grew along the roof and up the hill. Autumn leaves whirled around me in a dance. I took long deep breaths, soaking in the sights and smells of the crisp, deep woods before I would have to go back into the dark underground prison.

Hazella stood in the doorway with her familiar scowl. She tapped her foot and clenched a limber reed in her hand.

I made my expression solemn, bit my lip, and lowered my head.

Hazella swatted the reed across my legs. "Enough of yer lazy day dreamin'. There be no time ta waste, girl."

I repressed the sting and set the bucket next to the pile of firewood. The door to the back room hung open on its worn hinges. I peered into the forbidden room, trying to catch a glimpse of whatever mystery Hazella hid in there.

Hazella stepped in front of my gaze and slammed the door shut. Dirt sprinkled down from the ceiling. I lowered my head to protect my eyes from the debris. Hazella's wrinkled face flamed into a red scowl. The

witch waved her arms and shouted a line of profanities while pointing to things in the cottage that needed to be cleaned, refilled, or repaired.

"In the villages, they boil and behead people that be lazy, foolish, and troublemakin'." Hazella gripped the dull axe and hurled it at me. The heavy blade propelled through the air.

I dropped to the ground and covered my head with my hands. The axe whizzed past my ear and struck the rotting wall with a thud. Wood chips showered my hair and bounced off the dirt floor.

I looked at the axe, buried deep in the wood, and I clenched my hands into fists. The axe could easily have split my skull instead of imbedding itself in the wall.

Leaving the cottage during the winter didn't seem like such a bad idea after all. Frustration burned in my chest. I shouldn't be here and didn't deserve to be treated like an animal–worse than an animal. If my leg hadn't been injured, I would have run away last spring when I came to this wretched hole in the ground. I blinked hard and focused on fighting back angry tears. Crying only made Hazella irate.

"Ye must work extra hard today, girl," Hazella threatened. "I be havin' a delivery fer the villages tomorrow."

"A delivery?" I perked up. Was Hazella finally leaving me unguarded at the cottage? I wasn't strong enough to run away this time, but maybe when Hazella returned and saw me still at the cottage, she would leave me alone for a longer period next time. That's when I would escape.

Hazella pointed a withered finger at me. "If I don't get them potions ta the villages in time, people will die, and it'll be yer fault."

I rose to my feet, pressed my back to the wall next to the axe, and glanced at the door.

Hazella lunged forward and shook her fist in my face. "If ye wish ta

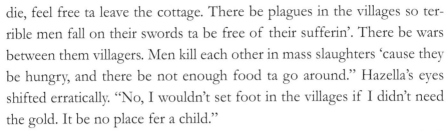

die, feel free ta leave the cottage. There be plagues in the villages so terrible men fall on their swords ta be free of their sufferin'. There be wars between them villagers. Men kill each other in mass slaughters 'cause they be hungry, and there be not enough food ta go around." Hazella's eyes shifted erratically. "No, I wouldn't set foot in the villages if I didn't need the gold. It be no place fer a child."

I clenched my jaw. The village I had come from wasn't that bad, although they did boil people they thought were witches . . . like me. A wave of hopelessness rushed over me as I remembered how I was betrayed by my own village. I bit my lip. My own village. I no longer had a home to escape to. I was truly alone. "I'm sorry," I murmured to Hazella.

"No, yer not. Yer never sorry." Hazella pulled a heavy book from the shelf above the fireplace. She flipped through the worn, yellowing pages and squinted to see the faded ink. She never bothered to re-scribe the book, because she wanted to destroy it after she memorized her recipes. Hazella muttered the words under her breath as she pointed to the shelf, "Fetch me them toad toes."

I limped to the shelf and retrieved a jar. Hazella examined the jar before sprinkling the toes into the bowl. I plugged my nose and squinted. Hopefully, I would never get sick with whatever this potion cured.

Hazella mixed the ingredients together. She poured it into a glass bottle before handing it to me. "Now put this in my bag fer the trip ta the villages."

I set the potion into the bag. "Is healing people your power?" I asked. It was an honest question. I didn't think Hazella would actually respond.

Hazella's eyes bulged unevenly. She turned to her book. "I can heal and destroy," Hazella murmured. "If I be an Immortal, I'd be ten times stronger than I am now. I wouldn't need this here necklace ta make me young."

I watched the ruby necklace swing like a pendulum as Hazella bent over the book. How could she think the necklace made her look young?

"I don't think the necklace is working," I said.

Wood grated against the hard-packed dirt as Hazella picked up a chair and threw it at me. I lunged to the side and huddled against the door. The chair hit the wall in an explosion of splinters. Several glass bottles fell from the shelves and shattered on the floor.

"But I be still strong," Hazella seethed. "It's what I have left of my hundred years of youth. I needs a new necklace." Hazella shook the necklace as if trying to get the last ingredients out of a glass bottle. "It be the easiest way I can become an immortal bride."

"You're engaged?" I asked. These were dangerous questions, but Hazella seemed to be giving information freely.

Hazella shook her head. "Not yet, but once I gets my young, powerful human body, I'll be stronger than even the Shadow Lords."

Chapter Four

Frost and Flame

Bright winter light shone through the window and reflected off the shelf of dusty jars like a rainbow chandelier. Snow blanketed the ground and blocked the roads to the villages.

"There didn't use ta be this much snow in England," Hazella complained. "Erebus be stealin' the heat of the earth to forge weapons for his army. You'll see. They be commin' soon, and I won't be standin' in their way."

I huddled in my bed of straw behind the stack of firewood. My frosty breath billowed into the air as I pulled a thin blanket around my head. I didn't understand a word of Hazella's disturbed statement. I wish I understood how crazy people's minds work, without having to go crazy myself.

I peered through a gap in the woodpile. Hazella sat next to the fireplace and stared at the flames while playing with a gold coin in her hand. I let out a long sigh. I hated winter. Not only was it cold, but Hazella never left the cottage. I was stuck in the same room with her until the snow melted.

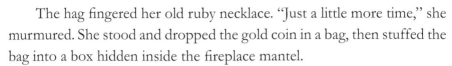

The hag fingered her old ruby necklace. "Just a little more time," she murmured. She stood and dropped the gold coin in a bag, then stuffed the bag into a box hidden inside the fireplace mantel.

I pulled the blanket tight under my neck. There was nothing special about the necklace. Hazella probably stole it off a dead person. She had a habit of robbing from graves.

I watched the shapes of my warm breath float into the chilly air. It was pathetic entertainment—but my only means to fight the monotony of winter.

A loud snort echoed through the cottage, followed by a heavy snore. I peered over the woodpile. The old woman finally fell asleep.

Hazella's book lay open on the table. My heart raced. I had to see inside. I couldn't read, but the pictures were in vivid color. I wanted to admire the art before Hazella destroyed the book to hide the secrets within.

I focused on the book and crept toward the table. My adventurous heart pounded. I placed my hands on the book. My fingers traced the scrolling art of thick brush strokes. Hazella snorted and stirred. I held my breath. The old woman rolled over and snored again. I exhaled, then turned the page.

I sighed and wondered what knowledge the book contained as I turned the thick yellowing pages. I lifted the last page and caught my breath. An image of the ruby necklace stared at me from the parchment. Its rich beauty seemed out of place among the images of herbs and animal parts.

Cold fingernails clamped onto my neck. My hands shot off the book like it was a poisonous serpent. My teeth snapped together. Hazella was going to kill me. I just knew it.

Hazella didn't say a word before she tossed me out into the deep forest snow and slammed the door shut.

The white world momentarily blinded me. I put my hands to my eyes. I jumped to my feet and pounded on the door. "Let me in!" I screamed.

Hazella ignored me and drew the curtains.

I knew it. She was feeding me to the wolves.

Trickles of warm blood ran down my neck where her nails had stabbed into me. The wind blew through my thin nightgown, chilling my skin. Every snowflake under my feet felt like needles pricking my red toes. I ran in place, lifting my aching feet from the frozen ground. The snow under me hardened. I slipped and fell onto the sharp ice.

"Ugh!" I cried out. Blood beaded on my scraped knees. Now, I was mad. I threw my fists into the snow and pounded at the ground. Even though I was hurt, I should've run away last summer.

I buried my face in my hands and cried. I hated feeling sorry for myself. I had been strong for so long. Now, repressed emotions of fear and anger surfaced. "I don't belong here. I don't deserve to die like this!" I wiped my face on the edge of my nightgown.

Through hot tears, I watched the winter world melt away. Warm mud plastered my legs and feet. Steam rose from the mud and surrounded me in a blanket of wet fog.

"What's happening?" I grasped a handful of autumn leaves, which had fallen before the winter snow buried them. In my hands, the leaves smoldered and burst into flames.

Golden flames billowed up my arms and danced in shimmering waves off my skin. I was on fire! My shriek echoed off the hills and the dead trees as surreal terror consumed me like the fire.

The mud on my legs dried to hard baked clay and flaked off onto

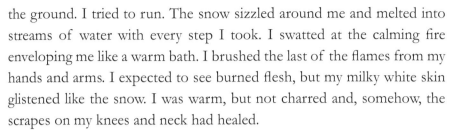
the ground. I tried to run. The snow sizzled around me and melted into streams of water with every step I took. I swatted at the calming fire enveloping me like a warm bath. I brushed the last of the flames from my hands and arms. I expected to see burned flesh, but my milky white skin glistened like the snow. I was warm, but not charred and, somehow, the scrapes on my knees and neck had healed.

I held my hands up and searched each finger one by one.

There was something wrong with me. Fire had spewed from my hands, and I wasn't burnt. If the superstitious witch knew what happened, she would suspect demonic power. "What sort of creature am I?" My hoarse whisper was thick with dread.

I shoveled snow over the warm ground to hide the evidence of my fiery outburst. My red fingers and toes ached for warmth again. How I wished for a cloak. The deep winter snow covered my feet and frost coated my eyelashes. I bit my lip and tucked my fingers under my arms next to my ribs. What if I didn't have to suffer? What if I could summon a little fire, just to keep my fingers and toes from freezing? The cottage curtains were still drawn. I pressed my ear to the door. Hazella snored deeply.

No one cared about me. If I was going to survive I would have to look after myself. I stiffened my lip and clenched my hands until my knuckles turned white. "I'll show her. I'm going to live!"

I grasped a fistful of leaves. Flames burst to life and danced in my hands. This wasn't normal. Fire was supposed to destroy whatever it touched—not heal. The flames skittered up my arms in showers of golden sparks. I tightened my jaw. What if I really was a witch like Hazella? What if Hazella was right and we were sisters of power?

My breath quickened. No. No matter what I was, I would never be like Hazella. I had to keep this power a secret until I discovered what was

wrong with me.

The wood slab barricading the door scraped open. I dispersed the flames, checked for any traces of ash, and faked a shiver. The door swung open.

I slumped my shoulders, keeping my arms around myself, and I hobbled inside toward my bed. I didn't dare turn and look at the witch for fear my expression would betray my secret. I leaped behind the woodpile onto the straw and threw the blanket around my shoulders.

Hazella pulled a red hot knife from the fire and demanded, "Give me yer frozen feet."

The old witch kept a jar of black fingers and toes on her shelf of potion ingredients. The jar was empty now, and obviously, she planned on harvesting more from me. I screamed and tucked my feet under my body.

Hazella snatched my right leg.

"No!" I shrieked and jerked away.

Hazella grabbed me and wrestled me to the ground.

I kicked and writhed. The heat of the knife brushed my leg as Hazella gripped my foot. "No!" I sobbed.

The witch released my leg. I pushed myself into the dark corner, tucked my knees to my chest, and covered my toes with my straining hands. Warm tears rolled down my cheeks and hit the dirt floor. "Please," I begged, "don't cut my toes off."

Hazella pointed the red knife at me. "Yer toes aren't frozen. How'd ye stay warm, girl?"

I wiped my face on my sleeve and thought fast. "Chimney," I muttered.

"Yer lyin'." Hazella dropped the knife in a bucket of water. The water sizzled as the knife landed with a thud at the bottom. Hazella raised one eyebrow, distorting her already hideous features. She leaned close and

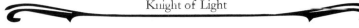

sniffed the air.

I quietly tested the air too, but could only smell Hazella's bad breath.

"Yer not covered in ash, but yer smellin' like smoke," Hazella mumbled. She kicked the bucket of water and turned the dirt floor into mud.

I repressed a smile that would've landed me back out in the cold. Adrenaline rushed through my veins, and my skin grew hot. I pressed my palms together to keep the fire of triumph from erupting out of my hands. I had finally gained a victory over Hazella.

Chapter Five

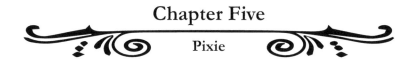

Pixie

August of spring air whirled through the underground cottage, distorting the firelight. Hazella entered and slammed the door. Loose debris showered down between the beams of dirt ceiling. The insane woman bounced across the room in a dance, happily singing. Her shrill voice sounded like a bag of feral cats.

I gripped the edge of the pot and soapy scrub brush. Hazella hadn't noticed me. Usually, she glowered over me or wandered in and out of her secret back room, making snide comments about my work in passing. This time, she hung her bag on a peg protruding from the wall above the fireplace.

The bag flopped back and forth on the peg. Whatever poor creature Hazella had caught struggled for life and shrieked like a teapot about to boil over. Images of frogs, dragonflies, and squirrels trapped in that bag came to my mind. Hazella always caught those types of creatures, but she never built cages for them. She usually killed them, or chopped off their

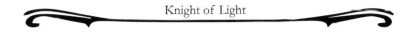

legs so they couldn't run away.

Hazella chanted inaudible words in a melodic rhythm as she gathered sticks, spider webs, and Shadow Wolf fur from her collection of ingredients. Hazella made a stick frame and meticulously weaved the spider's silk and wolf fur into a tight net around the box frame to make a cage.

The old witch put food and water in tiny thimbles and set them in the cage. She was feeding it. Whatever it was, she wanted it to live.

Hazella snatched the bag from the wall and shook it. "Quiet, you!" she said to the creature. Hazella eyed me. I quickly looked away and pretended not to care.

I couldn't understand. Why did she want this particular creature to live? For that matter, why was she still keeping me alive? There had to be a reason Hazella wasn't following her usual pattern of capture and kill.

The witch covered the cage with a rag to hide the creature from view. "I must leave quickly. Time be runnin' out." Hazella grabbed her bag and set a knife and glass vial on the table. "Girl, fill this now!"

I knew exactly what that meant. I clenched my teeth together, took the knife, and pierced the skin on the palm of my hand. I pressed around the wound to make the blood flow into the vial.

Hazella scowled. "Don't be selfish!" She reached for the knife. I grabbed it before she could and made the cut a hair deeper to increase the flow.

Hazella snatched the filled vial, put it in her bag, and prepared to leave while I bandaged my hand. She wouldn't say what for, but every week, she left the cottage with a vial of my blood, but this was the last time she would harvest anything from me.

I gasped under my breath, "Harvest." That was the only reason Hazella kept anything alive. I glanced at the rag-covered cage. What was

she harvesting from the poor creature?

Hazella pointed to the door. "Ye keep outta the cottage while I be gone. Ye hear now?"

I nodded, trying to look innocent and somber. Every cell in my body raced with adrenaline as I walked out the door. This was it. Not only would I escape, but I would liberate the creature in the cage as well. The strange fire that had enveloped me last winter had made my legs even stronger than before the wolf attack.

I picked up the axe, the one I would take to protect myself from the wolves, and I started chopping wood for the fireplace outside the cottage. Usually, Hazella forced me to stay in the cottage while she was gone. Obviously, this time she didn't trust me alone with the new creature.

Hazella hobbled down the path toward the villages with her bag of potions and my blood over her shoulder.

I pretended to do my chores and chopped wood until she was out of sight, then bounded to the edge of the clearing and watched Hazella amble around the bend. She was finally gone. I raced to the cottage, threw open the door, and dashed to the larder. I grabbed a few handfuls of bread and stuffed them into a bedroll.

I approached the cage and slowed my pace so I wouldn't startle the poor critter Hazella had caught. I lifted the cloth from the creature's cage.

Glittering silver light scattered across the tabletop.

A strange, but beautiful, creature looked at me with big azure eyes and pleaded, "Help Cassi! Please help poor Cassi!" Her voice chimed like bells.

I covered my mouth and stared at the tiny, winged girl. Her skin shimmered and antennae crowned her head of untamed, dark curls.

"What sort of creature are you?" I knelt beside the cage to get a

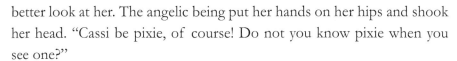

better look at her. The angelic being put her hands on her hips and shook her head. "Cassi be pixie, of course! Do not you know pixie when you see one?"

"No, I'm sorry. I've never seen a pixie before."

Cassi danced lithely toward me and grinned. "I Cassi, and you?"

"Auriella," I whispered. "I'm going to get you out of here."

Cassi nodded. "Auriella save Cassi from mean old witch?"

I blinked twice. It felt good to actually hear my name after being called "girl" for almost an entire year.

Though the pixie smiled, her face looked tired, and her wings drooped behind her back. If I had wings, I would have flown away from this place a long time ago.

"How did Hazella capture you?"

Cassi took a deep breath, and I could tell it was going to be a long story. "Cassi swimming with fish friends. Fish friends to Cassi. It's fairy treaty with water world. And Cassi splashing, and Cassi has no magic when wet and . . ."

"Hazella trapped you," I said, cutting Cassi's story short. I longed for the conversation, but there wasn't much time to escape.

"Yes." Cassi looked amazed that I knew how the story ended.

I leaned over the cage. "No door?"

Cassi shrugged her shoulders. Her wings glistened in the dim light from the fire, now burned to glowing coals. "If Cassi touch cage, spiders come."

I sighed. "Just because the cage is made of spiders' webbing doesn't mean spiders will come."

Cassi didn't look convinced.

"I wonder if there's a hidden door." I picked up the cage. Paralyzing

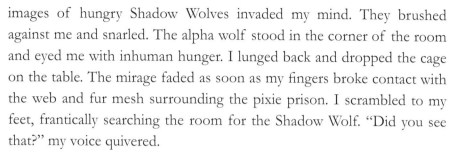

images of hungry Shadow Wolves invaded my mind. They brushed against me and snarled. The alpha wolf stood in the corner of the room and eyed me with inhuman hunger. I lunged back and dropped the cage on the table. The mirage faded as soon as my fingers broke contact with the web and fur mesh surrounding the pixie prison. I scrambled to my feet, frantically searching the room for the Shadow Wolf. "Did you see that?" my voice quivered.

Cassi looked around the room and raised one eyebrow. "See what?"

I stared at the web and fur. "It's a magic cage," I realized out loud.

Cassi bowed her head. "Mean old witch trap Cassi in scary cage."

I knelt and rested my chin on the tabletop. "Don't worry, Cassi. We'll find a way to get you out."

"Let's go now!" Cassi shook the stick frame and rattled the cage.

"Hazella is crazy, but not an idiot. Something awful might happen if we try to leave the cottage with you still inside the enchanted cage. We've got to find a way to open it or break the spell." I pressed on the edges of the stick frame, careful to avoid the web and fur mesh. "I wonder if it's some sort of puzzle."

The hours passed as I picked and prodded at the enchanted cage.

A tuneless song buzzed through the woods. I raced to the dusty window and peered outside. Hazella meandered along the path and stopped on occasion to add a plant or mushroom to her bag.

"She's coming," I whispered.

Cassi cowered in the corner of the unopened cage.

"When she leaves again, we will get you out," I promised and tossed the rag over the cage. I shoved the bread back into the cupboard, tucked the bedroll behind the firewood, and dashed to the door.

I fled outside to the small garden and picked at some weeds. What if

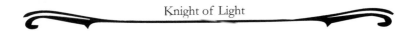

Hazella hid a key somewhere? Or maybe I needed to recite a riddle to get the cage to open? Hazella loved riddles. Everything she said and did was a riddle to me.

Hazella stood over me.

I burst out, in the best whining voice I could muster, "I'm so hungry. You didn't leave me any food, and I couldn't go into the cottage. Can I please eat something now?"

Hazella eyed me. My grip tightened on the weeds. I was sure Hazella knew I'd been inside.

Chapter Six

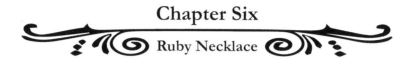

Ruby Necklace

I awoke and rubbed bits of the straw bed from my hair. Since I discovered Cassi last week, I spent every private moment searching for a key or trying to open the cage without one.

The dying fire lit the cottage with an eerie red glow. Hazella's bed lay empty, and the table where Cassi's cage usually rested stood vacant. Where could Hazella have taken Cassi in the middle of the night?

My heart dropped, and my stomach twisted. My fingers trembled as I searched the cottage for the pixie. What if I was too late and Hazella had killed Cassi?

Hazella's angry shout came from behind the door of the backroom. Candlelight beamed between the cracks. I dropped to my knees and peered through a crack in the door. I couldn't see Hazella or Cassi, but I heard the witch shout a furious string of threats.

From my peephole, I saw two sets of feet standing in the forbidden room. I covered my mouth to muffle my gasp. Someone else was here, but

no one ever came to the cottage, at least not on their own free will.

Hazella's book lay open on a tabletop, and she muttered instructions from a page. I distinctly heard the words: "gold," "pixie," and "ruby necklace." What did Cassi have to do with Hazella's old necklace? I tilted my head and tried to get a better look at the stranger. His hands moved as he talked. He was short and hairy, like a wolf, but he had the build of a man. Flickering candlelight distorted the features on his shadowy face.

Something the man said must have made Hazella mad because she let out a blood-chilling shriek and threw a bottle on the floor. I sprang to my feet as shards of sparkling glass sprayed under the door. I sprinted across the room and dove into my bed. My trembling hands clutched the blanket. My heart pounded so hard, I was afraid Hazella would hear it—like a warning drum to inform her of my snooping mischief.

The harder I tried to still my body, the more violently I quavered. The door to the back room creaked open. I pulled the blanket over my head and held my breath until the door closed again. I didn't dare fall asleep until later that night after the stranger left.

Two long days passed before Hazella departed for the villages and I could talk to Cassi in private.

"Oh, Cassi, are you all right? What did they do to you?"

Cassi's face lit up, and she sparkled even brighter. "Cassi so happy to see Auriella!"

I quickly evaluated the pixie. She still had her wings, limbs, and hair. I sighed with relief, then asked the next question weighing on my mind. "Who was that stranger?"

Cassi shrugged. "Cassi could not see. Mean old witch takes Cassi's dust and hide Cassi from big bad wolf-man."

"Wolf-man," I repeated uneasily. "We have to get out of here." I

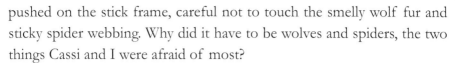

pushed on the stick frame, careful not to touch the smelly wolf fur and sticky spider webbing. Why did it have to be wolves and spiders, the two things Cassi and I were afraid of most?

"Try opening it from the inside," I instructed Cassi.

Cassi shook her head. "Cassi sees fairy friend get stuck in sticky web. Big spider comes and bites into fairy." Cassi wrung her hands together.

I softened my eyes. "Did this really happen?"

Cassi sat in the corner, pulled her knees close to her chest, and nodded.

"I'm so sorry. What was your friend's name?"

"Morning Dew." Cassi looked away and sighed. "Did wolfie eat Auriella's friend?"

I shook my head. "No, I was almost eaten by the wolves."

Cassi gasped.

"See these scars?" I brushed back my tangled hair and pointed to a faint scar on my temple. I lifted my ragged dress to show Cassi the jagged scar on my leg in the narrow crescent shape of a wolf's jaw.

Cassi's eyes were vivid with horror. "Auriella got away?"

"Hazella saved me. She said I owed her for saving my life. That's why I'm her slave." I paused, my brave façade melted, and tears welled in my eyes. "Sometimes I wonder if it would have been better if the wolves had eaten me."

Cassi stood and reached through the cage to pat my hair. "It's all right. Cassi help Auriella escape."

I lifted my eyes. "Cassi, your arm—. You can reach out!"

Cassi's wings fluttered. She grinned and pushed both arms out of the cage.

"The magic must be weakening." I wiped my face dry. "Let's try to open it now."

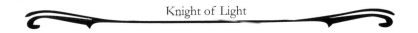

I closed my eyes and touched the cage, hoping it wouldn't still carry with it the frightening spell that had overwhelmed me the last time my hands had come in contact with it. I wasn't as lucky as Cassi, it seemed. As soon as my fingers brushed the bristly fur, images of a hungry pack sprang into life. I couldn't shut out the horrible vision. Fangs tore into my flesh. I screamed and clutched my calf. The illusion and pain dispersed when my hands left the cage. I pressed my palms over my eyes and groaned. I couldn't give up, I had to keep fighting. I stood, brushed myself off, and resolutely reached for the cage again.

"No!" Cassi shouted. "She's back!" Her glittering eyes widened, and she pointed out the window. Hazella's hunched-over figure ambled along the path.

I covered the cage with the cloth, picked up the axe, and raced outside. From the tall grass, I retrieved the extra wood I'd chopped the day before and tossed it into a heap. Though my heart raced, I casually hacked at a fallen tree near the cottage. Hazella fumbled with her bags full of goods from the village.

I drew my arm across my forehead and pretended to wipe away perspiration. Hazella scowled and looked at the pile of chopped wood before entering the cottage without saying a word.

I tottered with a phony limp as I piled the wood next to the cottage. My heart pounded in my ears. Would Hazella notice anything unusual in the cottage, something out of place? I restacked the woodpile and watched for any sign of movement from the window. If Hazella hadn't come to beat me by now, then I was probably safe.

I pressed the door open a crack and assessed the room. Hazella counted a stack of gold coins on the table. I looked away and pretended I hadn't noticed before limping toward the fireplace and dropping a log

onto the embers.

A hard knock resonated on the cottage door. Hazella and I both jumped. The old witch glared at me like I was the cause of this unexpected visit. Hazella's face grew as red as a boiled beet. My hands went cold, and my body froze in place like a statue of ice.

Hazella's eyes narrowed to a slit under her heavy lids. Her yellowing fingernails extended like claws. Hazella slapped me across the face. My cheek stung as it started to swell.

How could this unexpected visit be my fault? "I'm sorry." I apologized anyway and took a deep breath to calm myself so I wouldn't cry. If Hazella saw me crying, she would use the whip to punish me.

Hazella retrieved a crystal jar on the shelf. She filled her hand with cobalt powder and blew it into my face. I sneezed. What Hazella didn't know was that she had used the cobalt sleeping powder on me so often that I was immune to the effects.

I yawned and pretended to stumble toward the straw bed behind the woodpile. I placed the back of my hand to my forehead and let my knees give out.

Hazella opened the door. "What be ye doin' here? We agreed midnight!" Hazella shrieked, and I heard her slap the stranger.

The stranger mumbled something under his breath, then said audibly, "I finished the pendant of the necklace this morning and brought it right away, just as you asked." Though he sounded frightened, I recognized his deep voice and his footsteps when he entered the cottage. My eyes were wide open, but I resisted the urge to sit up and look at him. Through the cracks in the woodpile, I saw a dagger and a bag of tools on his leather belt. His long beard swept across the ground as he shifted his weight and wrung his hands.

"If yer ever surprisin' me, I'll be findin' another metal worker, and I'll use yer liver ta make a plague fer yer village."

"I need just a little more dust and I will have the last link done tomorrow," he said. Although his tone was pleasant, it sounded forced.

I bit my lip. The last link of the necklace would be done tomorrow? If the necklace could make Hazella stronger, I had to find a way to get Cassi out of the cage in less than twenty-four hours, or we would both be killed.

Chapter Seven

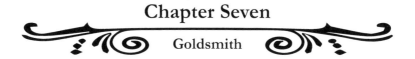

Goldsmith

I had to get away by morning, even if that meant using the secret fire inside me to burn down the cottage. Hazella would expect me to take the trail. There had to be another way through the dense, wolf-infested forest.

Hazella lifted a looking glass and smiled at her reflection. "It'll all be over soon." She ran her finger through the deep lines on her face. "Ye'll be beautiful again."

I gagged and rolled my eyes.

Hazella noticed me watching and pointed to the large black pot. "Clean this out! Yer always bein' lazy when there be work ta do. Soon ye won't be my problem anymore." She grumbled with the barest hint of a cruel smile.

I picked up a scrub brush and bar of lye. I dipped the brush into the remaining water and lathered it. Of course, I wouldn't be Hazella's problem anymore—once Cassi and I escaped. I clenched my teeth together and

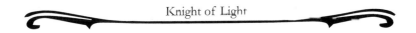

scrubbed the pot harder. After all I did to help, how could the decrepit old hag think of me as a problem?

I recalled the stranger saying he would return tonight with the last link for the necklace. For some reason Hazella didn't want me to know about him. The witch would probably try to use the cobalt sleeping powder on me again, or maybe she would try something stronger, like a sleeping stone.

"I needs some tea," Hazella demanded.

I stood and wiped my soapy hands on my dirty skirt. I picked up the bucket and headed for the door to get more water. Finally, a chance to go outside and scout for an escape route in the woods.

Hazella snatched the bucket from my hand. "I don't have time this mornin' fer a cripple. Ye walk like a three-legged horse on yer bad leg." Hazella marched outside and slammed the door behind her.

This was even better—alone in the cottage at last. I dashed to Cassi and tore the cloth off the cage. Cassi beamed, and I put my finger to my lips. "We need to find a way to distract Hazella and get out of here before the hairy-man comes back. I might have to set the cottage on fire. It could be dangerous."

Hazella's shadow sped past the window. Her furious stride was all I had to see to know that the witch heard us talking. My heart dropped like an iron weight into my stomach. I knelt next to Cassi and gripped the table. My eyes darted around the room for someplace to hide, but I couldn't move. Terror paralyzed me, locking me in place.

Hazella stood in the doorway. Her face grew from red to purple, making her hair look grayer. "Come here, girl!" she snarled.

There was nowhere to hide and no way to escape—I had to fight.

I took a weak stance as if ready to fight. Hazella screamed with

laughter. "Ye have no idea who yer dealin' with." The witch picked up a broom and snapped it in half over her knee. "I be the righteous one. I saved ye from Erebus's Shadow Wolf. And once I finds out what yer power is, I'll be negotiatin' with him fer my reward."

Hazella gripped both my wrists with one hand; her fingernails pierced my skin. "I be tired of yer games. What did Erebus want with ye?"

I shook my head, trying to clear the confusion and terror clouding my thoughts. "Erebus? Shadow Wolf?" I stammered, "I don't know! I told you it was a mistake. I'm just an orphan—no one special."

Hazella squeezed my wrist with a crushing grip and tied my hands to the peg over the fireplace mantel. "This be yer last chance." Hazella retrieved a long whip with frayed edges. "Does Erebus want to be drinkin' the blood runnin' through yer veins? What is so special about ye?"

"Please," I begged. My breath quickened and my muscles tensed. "I don't know anything about Erebus." Tears leaked down my face as I pressed my eyes shut. "No, please, don't."

Crack!

The whip snapped over my head and lashed onto my back, cutting deep into my flesh. I tried not to scream.

"Are ye human or Neviahan?" she asked.

"I'm human!" I shrieked. The old woman had gone mad. "Look at me, I'm human!" I was about to say, "I'm human like you," but I wasn't anything like Hazella.

"That's what they all be sayin'." The whip snaked through the air and sliced across my exposed skin.

Nothing I said would stop Hazella from her erratic attack. I leaned my head against the stone, trying to relax my body and think of something else besides what was happening to me. Though pain seared me,

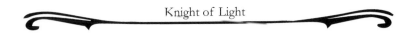

I imagined a magical kingdom far away and lost myself in the glory of a perfect day. The sun peaked over the low rolling hills and showered golden strains of light through a valley of freedom.

"Have the Immortals seen ye? Have ye been trained by them nasty Neviahan druids?"

Her voice pulled me, like a hooked fish, out of the water of my hallucination, and I gasped for breath. I didn't understand the witch's riddles. My head spun, and I stammered, "I don't know what—"

"LIAR!"

The strikes came faster now, as the whip seemed to take its own delight in my suffering. Warm blood trickled down my cold skin as the whip raked my delicate flesh. My fingernails dug into the wood mantel. I gasped for air between each strike, hopelessly searching for the strength to fight back, then silently begging for the escape that now eluded me. My legs gave out, and I dangled by my wrists. I held my breath and refused to moan or let her win.

"What powers do ye have that Erebus craves?" Hazella shouted.

I gasped for air to breathe. Even if I had been able to talk through the pain, I wouldn't have revealed what I knew. I would never tell the witch about the fire that sprang from my body last winter.

The whip hacked mercilessly at my body. My dress hung in shreds off my shoulders and hip, but Hazella kept ranting and swinging the whip.

"I be havin' my own ways of findin' out. If yer Neviahan, ye will survive the night. If yer nothing but a human, then I will discard yer remains for the wolves."

I imagined wings like Cassi's, sprouting out of my back where my skin ripped open. The pain didn't seem so bad then. Blood fell like thick raindrops onto the dirt floor and splattered against the fireplace.

My body pulsed with pain. I could still feel the whip carving my flesh from my bones, even after Hazella finished beating me.

She took a long drink and dabbed the sweat from her forehead. She untied me from the peg, and my beaten body fell to the ground like a sack of butchered meat.

I lay on my stomach, straining against the pain. Every breath I inhaled and exhaled hurt. The witch placed some cold vegetable soup on the floor beside me. "Now eat!"

Eating was the last thing I could think of doing. My body felt disconnected and full of holes.

Hazella moved away, pulled out her knife, and ran it meticulously across a smooth river stone.

She'd said the only way I would last the night was if I were a Neviahan. What other tortures did she have planned?

The light from the fire reflected on something in my soup, something blue. My eyes fluttered, trying to see more clearly. I tried to think of anything in the cottage edible and blue.

Hazella turned her back, and I fished out the brilliant turquoise sleeping stone. I gripped it in my fist. This was it—the way I would escape. I choked down a few bites of soup and moaned, "I am so tired." I pretended to yawn for effect.

"I haven't had my tea yet," Hazella complained.

I was in greater pain and was more delirious than when the wolf had attacked me and, yet, Hazella was ordering me to get her tea?

"Hurry, I be havin' important business tonight." The witch's voice sounded eager—too eager. Hazella continued to sharpen her murdering knife. The metal screeched as it slid against the rock.

I pushed myself to my feet and stumbled against the wall toward

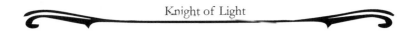

the pot of water over the fireplace. Shaking, I tried to ignore the blood running down my arms and legs. Now I knew why I wouldn't be Hazella's "problem" anymore. She planned to murder me or turn me over to Erebus's wolves.

I clenched my teeth together. It was tempting to take the sleeping stone myself and be free of the pain, but Hazella wasn't going to win this time. I discreetly dropped the turquoise pebble in the bottom of her cup and poured the boiling water over it. I waited until the stone dissolved before straining the tea leaves.

I held out the cup to Hazella. The old witch snatched it from my hand and moaned with exhaustion, like she was the victim of the whipping.

Not needing to exaggerate, I limped weakly to my bed and dropped onto my stomach. I pulled at my tattered dress so the cloth wouldn't stick to my wounds. My fingers strained as I fought against the pain. I looked through the woodpile at Hazella sipping on her tea. Her head nodded, her eyes closed, and the tea cup fell to the ground. She looked like a lifeless rag doll asleep in her chair.

Finally, I could use my powers to stop the pain. Flames sprang from my clenched hands and danced on my skin like oil on water. The warm blaze from my hands ignited the straw. Perspiration dripped from my face as the soothing blanket of warmth enveloped me and eased my pain.

The fire died around me and I lay naked in the bed of ashes. The pain from the whipping seemed like only an intense memory. I shrugged my shoulders and rubbed my hands over the deep scars on my back. At least the wounds were closed up, and I wasn't going to die tonight. I pulled a fresh nightgown over my head and wished I had something else to wear.

Cassi sobbed. "Oh, poor Auriella."

I put my finger to my lips. "I'll be fine. Let's get you out of this cage

so we can leave this place forever."

A heavy knock fell on the door. Through the clouded window, the silhouette of the hairy man moved outside the cottage.

I held the cage close to my chest and dove for my ashen bed behind the woodpile.

The knocks on the door rapped faster and louder. "It's I, Ruburt. Let me in."

I turned to Cassi and whispered, "Ruburt. He's the stranger who is making the necklace for Hazella, and he's just as bad as the witch if he's her friend."

The handle on the door clicked. The hinges squealed open, and the stranger tiptoed like a bandit into the cottage.

I peered from behind the pile of wood. The bearded stranger gripped his dagger and searched the room. He noticed Hazella asleep in the chair and shook her. "Hazella! I have the last link of your necklace."

I bit my lip. Hazella wasn't going to awaken anytime soon. Those sleeping stones made people sleep for days.

Ruburt wrinkled his face and looked frightened. "What spell is cast on this place?"

"He thinks I've cast a spell," I whispered to Cassi.

Cassi covered her mouth and shook with silent laughter.

Ruburt swung around and faced the pile of wood. He held out his dagger. "Whoever you are, come out and show yourself!"

Chapter Eight

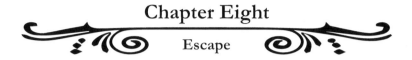

Escape

There was no use in hiding, and I wasn't going to let him, or anyone, stop me from escaping. I stood firmly and eyed the short man who called himself Ruburt.

He lowered his dagger, but his dark eyes kept a sharp gaze on me. "Who are you?" he demanded.

"Who are you?" I retaliated. "Are you some sort of overgrown hairy pixie?"

He coughed like he was choking back laughter. "I ain't no pixie. I'm a dwarf. Now, who are you? Some sort of witch in training?"

"Of course not. I am Auriella. I live here, but not for much longer."

Ruburt scoffed, "I've come here many times before, and I've never seen you."

"I've seen you and know all about you." I tilted my head and tried to sound intimidating, especially since he didn't know anything about me. I glanced at Cassi who smiled and nodded.

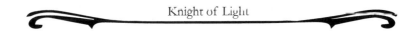

Ruburt raised a bushy eyebrow. "If that were true, you would've at least had the sense to know I'm not an overgrown pixie. Now, who are you really? What've you done to the old witch? What's wrong with her?"

"She is in a deep sleep and will not awaken for a whole day."

"You're a witch too! You've cast a spell on her!" The dwarf pointed his dagger at me.

I placed my hands on my hips. "I am not a witch! I'm not anything like Hazella. I won't ever be like her! I gave her something to make her sleep. In a day or two from now, she will awaken and be fine."

"I don't believe you," Ruburt said quickly. "But you don't look like a witch. You're too . . . pretty."

"Me?" I gasped in disbelief and braced myself on the woodpile. No one but my parents had ever called me pretty before.

The dwarf frowned and nodded.

"I'm pretty?" I couldn't believe it. After all that I had been through, someone actually thought I was pretty. I touched my face and brushed back my tangled hair.

"Don't let it go to your head. You're absolutely filthy." The dwarf wrinkled his nose. "And you smell like the old witch too." Ruburt slid his dagger back into the scabbard.

I clenched my teeth and heat rose from my fingertips. "Who are you? Are you Hazella's friend?"

"Humph, I wouldn't be her friend if she was the last breathing creature on this Earth. She's forcing me to make a new necklace for her. Its finished, and I'm ready to be done with that old hag."

I softened my face and unclenched my fist, allowing the blood to flow back into my white knuckles.

"My name is Ruburt. I'm a goldsmith from the dwarf village."

"Dwarf village?"

"Yes, it's far away from all the other villages." Ruburt crossed his arms in front of his burly chest. "It's where people with dwarfism can live in peace."

"Hmmm." I tapped my lips with my finger thoughtfully. "I have a friend who is little too. Maybe you can help us escape, and we can come with you."

Ruburt's eyes darted around the room. "Another little person? Here?"

I nodded, and using the cloth like an oven mitt, I lifted Cassi's cage.

Ruburt stepped back and stroked his long beard. "A pixie. So this is how Hazella got the dust." He scowled and looked disgusted. "Pixie dust was molten into the gold links of the new necklace." He reached into his pocket and held a thin gold ring pinched between his fingers. "After I give her this last link and get my money, I am never doing work for a witch again." Ruburt kicked the leg of Hazella's chair. The witch didn't stir. "I'm not leaving without my pay."

"How much did she say she would give you?" I glanced at the fireplace mantel where the witch hid her coins.

"Ten times the weight of the necklace, in gold."

Hazella would never part with that much gold. Now I knew why Hazella sharpened that old knife—she planned on killing Ruburt. "If you help us escape and lead us away from here, I will pay you what the witch promised."

Ruburt froze as if holding his breath. He eyed me, then looked at Hazella. "Now, you've trapped me."

"How?" I grimaced again at the thought of being anything like Hazella.

"If I don't help you, I won't get paid, and you will tell the old witch

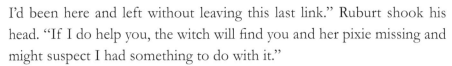

I'd been here and left without leaving this last link." Ruburt shook his head. "If I do help you, the witch will find you and her pixie missing and might suspect I had something to do with it."

Ruburt put his fingers to his mouth and started gnawing on his nails. His eyes darted from the witch back to me several times. Finally, he dropped his shoulders. "Fine, what do you need me to do?"

I set Cassi's cage on the table. "I can't get the pixie out. I've pulled at the sticks and looked for a door."

"Let me examine the cage." Ruburt picked up the cage with his bare hands, but didn't react to the magic.

"Oh, Cassi want out!" the pixie pleaded.

Ruburt smiled his first genuine smile. He turned the box in his hands. "It's simple. Why can't you figure out how to open the cage?"

"It's magical," I informed him.

"It doesn't seem magical to me. Why doesn't the pixie just fly out?"

"Cassi trapped in cage!" the pixie cried and rattled the stick frame.

"Cage?" Ruburt scoffed, "This is not a cage. It's a couple of sticks with spiders' webbing and wolf fur strung between 'em. If the wind blew hard enough, it could break."

I shook my head. It certainly looked like a cage, and Cassi couldn't get out.

"Go on, Auriella. Free the pixie," Ruburt encouraged.

"But how?" I dropped my arms to my sides. "I want to, but I don't know how."

Ruburt raised his eyebrow. "You don't seem like a half-wit. Why can't you figure it out?" He picked up the cage and stroked his beard thoughtfully. "Are you afraid of wolves?"

My hands trembled. "How did you know?"

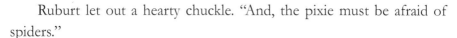

Ruburt let out a hearty chuckle. "And, the pixie must be afraid of spiders."

Cassi shrieked and huddled in the corner of the cage.

Ruburt placed the cage on the table. "The only thing that's stopping you is your own fears. All you have to do is tear the wolf's fur and spider webbing from the stick frame."

I bit my lip and wrung my hands together. It was too easy. What if one of the wolves really came to life after Cassi was freed and ate us both? I took a deep breath. I didn't know what would happen, but I had to try something. Ruburt nodded and winked, which gave me encouragement. I lifted my hand and pressed against the cage.

The Shadow Wolf stepped through a pillar of billowing smoke. It's not real, I reminded myself. The wolf dashed forward. My heart thumped wildly. The ground shook. The beast snarled, revealing a row of glistening teeth. I tightened every muscle in my body and resisted the urge to run.

"You can do it Auriella!" Ruburt shouted.

I had to stand firm and stop these illusions of fear or Cassi and I would be trapped forever. The beast charged forward and sprang toward me. Its mouth opened wide, its claws reached to tear me apart. I swung my fist and sliced through the illusion.

"Cassi be free! Cassi be free!" The pixie flew from the cage and danced in the air.

I caught my breath and turned to Ruburt. "Thank you."

Ruburt's lips pulled into a smile. He cleared his throat and regained his solemn expression.

Cassi flew to the fireplace and shouted, "Help! Help, Cassi!"

"What is it now?" Ruburt furrowed his brow. "Is the pixie always getting into trouble like this?"

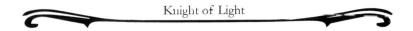

Cassi put her hands on her hips. "Cassi wants dust back!"

I removed the stone from the fireplace mantel where Hazella had hidden her treasure.

"What's this?" Ruburt asked and stroked his long beard.

I took the first bag from the hiding spot and dropped it on the table-top. The unmistakable sound of coins clanked together. My fingers trembled as I struggled to undo the knot in the leather strings.

Ruburt reached across the table and grabbed the bag from me. "Let me do it!" He untied the knot and picked up the bag, pouring the contents on the top of the table. Ruburt licked his lips and ran his fingers through the coins. He raced to the fireplace, brought the other three bags to the table and dumped out their contents. From the last bag, the unfinished necklace fell onto the heap of gold.

Cassi landed on the table next to the treasure. "Necklace made with Cassi's dust."

Ruburt looked at me. "I will lead you out of here, but first, I will take my fair price for what the witch owes me."

The pixie buzzed around his head. "Take Cassi too! Take Cassi too!"

"Of course, I will take both of you. Now gather your things and let's go. It's getting late, and we need to be a long way from here before the old witch awakens. She will be furious, especially when she finds you both gone and her treasure missing too."

Ruburt scooped the coins into the bags, and I put all I could carry into an old bedroll.

My heart welled with excitement for adventure and freedom. Things were going to be better once I reached the dwarf village. I might even get to learn how to read.

Ruburt placed the heavy coin bags over his shoulders. "Then let's get

outta here."

We stepped out of the cottage into the cold night air. I grabbed the axe and pinned it under the door handle.

"Good idea," Ruburt said. "That should buy us a little more time before Hazella starts following us."

"I was thinking," I started, and hoped Ruburt would take advice from a fourteen-year-old girl, "we should follow the stream instead of the trail so we will be harder to track."

"Brilliant," Ruburt said.

I smiled. I was running away with, quite possibly, the two last decent people on Earth.

Cassi and I followed Ruburt along the stream bed. After a few miles, the stream flowed into a meadow pond. Several trails led across a meadow and into the dense woods.

I glanced around the foreign landscape. "Where to now?" I asked.

"North," Ruburt said and led us onward.

I studied the strange little man from behind. The top of his balding head reflected the moon as he walked with short uneven steps on his stout legs. Ruburt mumbled to himself and bit at his fingernails. He marched a few paces ahead of me. The bags of coins bounced on his back with each step he took. After traveling several miles, I edged closer to hear his mumblings.

"Hazella was asleep when we left her. She won't know I'd been there . . . or will she? She's a witch, and witches have ways of finding things out." He slowed, adjusted the bags, and resumed his stride. "What am I to do? Should I go home? Drats! The old witch knows where I live. Eventually she will come for me. She might send a plague to my village if she knows I'm there." He stopped dead in his tracks, and I almost ran into him.

I pretended to be interested in the blue stars overhead and hoped he didn't notice me eavesdropping. Cassi flew to me, tilted her head, and scrunched her eyebrows. I placed a finger over my lips then pointed at the dwarf. Ruburt continued to hike along the trail. I scuffled behind him.

"That's what witches do . . . it is . . . don't fool yourself, Ru," Ruburt said to himself. "Terrible things happen to people who deceive 'em. Something awful like leprosy, or boils, or heaven forbid–marriage!"

I smiled to myself. Dwarves were indeed strange creatures. My bare foot hit a rock. I stumbled and flew into the back of Ruburt, causing him to drop the bags. He scowled at me.

"I'm sorry." I helped Ruburt gather the bags.

The anger didn't last long on his weary face. He looked around the secluded place along the path. "Here," Ruburt said as he stretched his neck to one side. "We shall rest. Dwarves weren't made to climb mountains and hills; we were made to dig through 'em."

The wind howled. The hair on my arms stood on end. An eerie chill ran down my spine like cold water. I imagined myself awakening to see the witch standing over me with a whip and a red hot knife.

"Let's go a little farther." I clenched my bedroll to my chest and scanned the shadowy woods. I couldn't help but feel that someone or something from the forest watched us.

Ruburt found several large stones and arranged them in a circle for a fire.

I hesitated before dropping my bedroll on the ground. I dove inside and covered my head.

Ruburt chuckled low in amusement. "If you're really that scared, you can gather some firewood so we can have some light."

Like a child, I wanted to stay huddled under my bedding.

"Come, Auriella." Cassi encouraged. "Cassi help Auriella."

I peered from the covers to see Cassi fluttering through the air like a cheerful star.

A smile tugged at my lips. I pulled myself to my feet and followed Cassi.

The pixie flew back and forth through the woods calling, "Be this good stick for fire? Oh, how about this one?" Cassi held a tiny pixie-size twig.

"No, no, Cassi." I giggled. "That one would be burnt in a second. We need bigger ones, like this." I lifted a long, dead branch.

I returned to camp with my arms full of the firewood that we had found. Ruburt gathered a few dead leaves and started the fire.

"Stay here," Ruburt instructed. He tucked his dagger into the scabbard on his belt.

"Where are you going?" I couldn't believe he planned to leave us alone with only a campfire to ward off the creatures of the woods.

"To find food," was the only answer he gave before disappearing from sight.

Cassi and I sat next to the fire and watched the unfamiliar woods.

Shadows danced off the spiny trees as the fire flickered back and forth. The burning logs snapped in the heat. My lungs froze. For a moment I stopped breathing, but my heart raced erratically. Dark clouds rolled in, veiling the night lights in the sky. I fed the fire several times to keep it burning. Ruburt still had not returned. What if something awful happened to him? What if the wolves tracked us and attacked? The wind moaned through the treetops.

"Did you hear that?" I barely moved my mouth, but my eyes widened with terror.

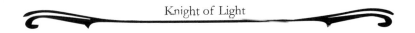

"Sounds like spiders," Cassi whispered.

"Spiders," I stuttered. "Sounds like wolves to me." The treetops cracked. A gale whirled around me and threatened to extinguish our weakening fire. Tall grass swooshed against my arm. I leapt to my feet and frantically brushed my skin.

"Something touched me. It felt like a spider or maybe a—" My voice quivered and paralyzed my tongue from speaking. The wolves were close, I just knew it. The dark forest swayed. The wind howled, giving me an even stronger sense that hungry wolves were waiting for me in the underbrush of the forest, just off the path. I crouched low to the ground and slid closer to the fire. Pulling the bedroll over my head, I peered out a small opening. Cassi clung to me like a leech.

"Something's coming," Cassi whimpered. I saw it too. The silhouette of a large hairy beast emerged from the woods. Heavy, hot breaths puffed into the cold night air as it growled.

Chapter Nine

Ambush

The swelling terror burst inside me. I let out a high-pitched shriek and jumped to my feet.

"Are you tryin' to give this poor dwarf a heart attack?" Ruburt stepped into the light and put his hand to his heart.

"Ruburt!" I shouted. My knees hit the ground. I bent over to catch my breath. "It's only you."

Ruburt put his finger to his lips, hushing me. "Do you want every dark creature in the forest to hear us?" Ruburt growled. "You two are so worked up 'bout wolves and spiders when we should be worried 'bout Hazella."

I shook my head. "Why did you leave us?"

"I thought we should eat something other than bread. I caught us a fish." He placed his skewered catch over the flames.

Cassi screamed and flew into a tree. "Ruburt is big, mean fish-killer!"

Ruburt ignored her and added more wood to the fire.

I couldn't bring myself to eat someone who might have been Cassi's friend. "I think I'll stick with bread."

"You need more than bread and water." Concern flickered in Ruburt's eyes.

"I'm used to it," I reassured him. I wouldn't take any chance of offending Cassi, even if I went a little hungry.

Ruburt grunted. "If the wind blows any harder, it'll sweep you off your feet. I can tell Hazella didn't feed you like she should've." He rotated the fish over the fire.

I took a few small bites from a hard loaf of bread.

"We need to keep our strength. The rebel army hides in these woods," Ruburt warned. "Erebus and his thugs."

The Shadow Legion. I recognized the name of the Shadow King. Hazella had muttered Erebus's name in reverence during storms and on foggy days.

Bitter wind blew past me. Shivers trickled down my spine like icy claws. I recalled Hazella saying something about Erebus, the one who sent the Shadow Wolf to kill me. Perhaps he knew of my abnormality and wanted me dead because of it. Creating fire wasn't my fault. It just happened, and I didn't plan on ever doing it again. I just wanted to be normal.

Ruburt continued, "The villagers think they're demons. Personally, I don't think even demons are capable of the carnage the Shadow Legion leaves behind. They're something else, chameleons with the darkness and sometimes disguised as their own prey—humans."

My chest rose and fell rapidly. "What do they do to people?" I asked, but didn't know if I really wanted to know.

Ruburt laughed without humor. "Nothing I'll say in front of a lady." He pulled the fish from the fire and offered me half.

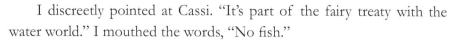

I discreetly pointed at Cassi. "It's part of the fairy treaty with the water world." I mouthed the words, "No fish."

"Humph." He took a bite out of the fish's flesh and chomped on it. "I'm no fairy."

I pressed my bedroll against my chest and watched the forest for any sign of movement. "Is there anything we can do to stop the rebels?" I asked.

Ruburt grunted. "The only thing humans can do is resist the Shadow Legion's temptations 'cause that's how they take over. They bait humans in by offering power and comfort then, WHAM! It's over. It's like this fish." He pointed to the remains on the stick. "All I had to do was hook a worm on the line to bait it in." He licked his fingers. "Now I've consumed the fish's body, just like the Shadow Legion disposes of humans. As long as humans keep taking the bait, the Rebellion will survive."

My stomach turned. I pinched my nose and covered my mouth to muffle the smell of the fish.

"Now the Neviahans, that's another story." Ruburt put his hands behind his head and kicked off his boots. "Them Neviahans can take out a whole legion of Shadow Spirits. Some of them Immortal Neviahans can even kill a Shadow Lord. I heard that when the Lady of Neviah comes, even Erebus, himself, will be afraid of her."

I looked down at my hair and picked at the split ends. "What do you think the Lady of Neviah is like?"

"Donno," Ruburt answered. "She's a warrior, so she's gotta be strong." Ruburt used one of the fish bones to pick at his teeth.

I secretly admired the woman that I had never met. I knew very little about her, but I knew that she was everything I wasn't. The Lady of Neviah was strong and fearless. She wouldn't be afraid of anyone,

especially not someone like Hazella or a Shadow Wolf.

"Auriella, do you know what the ruby necklace is for?" Ruburt's question caught me off guard.

I shrugged. "I'm not sure. Hazella talked about it renewing her body so she can get married."

Ruburt held his breath, his eyes bulged, then he erupted in laughter. "That's why Hazella seemed so eager to have it. I wonder what's going to happen to the old hag, since Cassi insisted on taking it."

"Not mean old witch's," Cassi defended. "Necklace made of Cassi's dust." A proud smile played on the pixie's face.

"What does pixie dust do?" Ruburt wondered out loud.

A blue spark flew from Cassi's fingers at Ruburt's beard, making it curl into lovely locks. "It zaps fish-killers."

I muffled my giggle.

Ruburt mumbled and gave Cassi a sideways glance. "Are you still mad about the fish?" He tried to smooth and straighten his beard without much luck.

"No, Cassi feel much happier now." The pixie flashed a toothy smile.

Ruburt mused, "Well, why would the witch want pixie dust in the necklace?"

I smirked. "Maybe to curl her hair?" Cassi and I burst into laughter, and even Ruburt chuckled a little. I loved it when I could say witty things.

Ruburt rose to his feet and arched his back into a stretch. "Well, we can either stay here for tonight or keep moving."

"Keep moving," I said without question. I wanted to be far away by the time Hazella awoke. Besides, after Ruburt's talk about the Rebellion, I wouldn't sleep.

"Stay," Cassi said. "Cassi so sleepy. Cassi cannot see in dark. Might

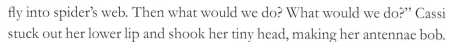

fly into spider's web. Then what would we do? What would we do?" Cassi stuck out her lower lip and shook her tiny head, making her antennae bob.

"You'll be all right. You'll be all right," Ruburt repeated in a mocking tone. He lifted the coins and grunted.

I pulled my cloak closed to hide my nightgown. "I know you are strong, but if you'd like me to help carry something, I can," I offered, trying not to hurt his pride.

"Oh," Ruburt shrugged, "are you sure?"

I nodded.

Ruburt handed me two of the four bags of coins. "It will help us make better time."

I took the two bags of coins, tied the strings together and placed them around my shoulders. I squirmed under the weight of the coins. They were heavier than they looked.

I followed behind Ruburt and focused on the trail. The moonlight broke through the clouds and lit the path. The cool earth chilled my exposed toes as I stepped carefully around every sharp stone. I gripped my cloak tighter under my chin.

It didn't seem long before the first light of day painted the sky with pastel hues. The sun rose over the hills and higher into the sky.

I took in the beauty of the surrounding woods. The trees here were different. We must have passed from one forest to the next during the night. Instead of branches fanned out in dusty green boughs, the glossy leaves shimmered in the sunlight whenever a breeze rustled them. I scanned the misty valley below before closing my eyes and taking in a deep breath. Despite all the walking, this was much better than being at the cottage.

"Don't get too comfortable," Ruburt said. I opened my eyes to see

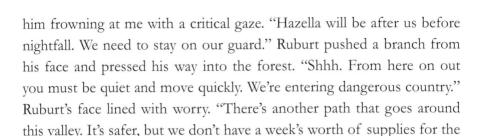

him frowning at me with a critical gaze. "Hazella will be after us before nightfall. We need to stay on our guard." Ruburt pushed a branch from his face and pressed his way into the forest. "Shhh. From here on out you must be quiet and move quickly. We're entering dangerous country." Ruburt's face lined with worry. "There's another path that goes around this valley. It's safer, but we don't have a week's worth of supplies for the journey. I hadn't planned to go this far in the first place."

I never intended to put him in danger. I cringed at my own selfishness. The sooner we got to the village, the better off Ruburt would be. At least we were making better time today through a lush forest of willow trees and overgrown fern.

"This is Clun Forest," Ruburt whispered as if someone else could be listening. His eyes darted around the woods. Sunlight glittered through the canopy of leaves in brilliant patches, and butterflies floated from one bright flower to the next.

"What is so bad about this forest?" I asked.

Ruburt put his finger to his lips, hushing me. He spoke again in a mute whisper, "The elves and fairies live here. It's heavily protected 'cause the elves don't like outsiders. The fairies also set traps for trespassers. We must be out of their territory by nightfall. Tonight, we'll be near a town called Oswestry."

"Is this where you live, Ruburt?"

"I live in the Golden Valley, where all the other dwarves live." He sounded somewhat annoyed, but at least he answered my question.

"Do you have children?" I asked sociably.

"Nope!" The volume of his hasty reply startled me. "I need to find a wife first, and I'm not interested in looking for one."

"Are they hard to find?" It sounded like a silly question, but I didn't

know how many dwarf women existed.

Ruburt paused. His body shook. I couldn't tell if he was angry or laughing. "I just haven't had the time to look, and I don't think I'll be going back to my village." Sadness droned in his voice.

"Why not?" I asked.

Ruburt started to mumble something about the witch and a plague. I didn't catch all of what he said, but by his tone, I could tell it wasn't good. Of course he couldn't return to his village. Hazella was probably on her way there now. I bit my lip. Ruburt not only put his life in danger to help me, but he left behind his people and everything he owned.

The path narrowed and disappeared altogether, but we continued to trudge through the dense forest. The thick treetops bore down on me with claustrophobic malice and blocked out the sunlight. Cassi glowed like a torch, lighting the way through the jungle of fern, willow, ash, and oak. I wrapped my arms around my middle. If I had any accidents with my fire in this forest, half of England would burn.

Cassi gasped and pointed at a ring of mushrooms along our path. "It be fairy trap."

Ruburt stepped around it. "We don't want to get caught in one of those."

I eyed the colorful mushrooms. "Why not?"

The pixie sang and lithely fluttered along the path.

"Trapped in fairy ring for a thousand years,
You will not sleep, you will not eat,
But, you'll dance to the fairy's waltz."

She stopped singing and added, "Cassi good at this game."

I tiptoed over the fairy ring. "It's a good thing we have Cassi to help us avoid these traps."

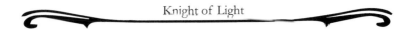

Ruburt nodded in agreement.

Cassi spun through the air and chanted,

"They fell out of bed and landed on their head
'Cause they stepped on our flowers and mocked our powers
Now they're dancing to the fairy's waltz."

The tune was catchy and I found myself singing with Cassi.

"We'll spook your horse and tease your cat
By the shadows we make on the barnyard wall."

"Come on, Ruburt, sing with us." I laughed.

The dwarf hummed low at first, then added to our chorus in his deep voice:

"We'll raid the oatmeal chest and steal the brightest cherries.
Why do you put your fallen teeth under the pillows while you sleep?
We'll steal those too, and hide one shoe, then wait to see what you do."

We sung faster and louder. I spun in circles and Ruburt kept time with his hands.

"Pull the pins from your favorite dress as it dries out in the sunshine.
Tickle your nose as you sleep and bite your mule like a swarm of fleas.
If you lose your way, you'll never get back, stuck in our enchanted fairy trap.
You will not sleep, you will not eat, but forever be dancing to the fairy's waltz."

Ruburt stopped clapping and looked around the woods with narrowed eyes. "Wait a minute, something's wrong. How do we all know this ridiculous song?"

Cassi and I continued to sing and blithely dance.

"Fairy magic," Ruburt huffed. "No good can come from that deadly

art. The fairies are not a race to trifle with."

I spun and halted in my tracks. A fairy wand pressed against the tip of my nose.

Ruburt's face turned chalky white. He held up his hands in a surrendering gesture.

One of the hundreds of fairies surrounding us held the wand at my nose like a sharpened sword.

Cassi continued to prance through the air.

I waved my arm to get the pixie's attention. "Shhh, Cassi, stop singing."

"Huh?" Cassi asked.

"Do not try to run away—unless you wish to become rabbits," a petite, yet muscular, fairy man threatened.

Chapter Ten

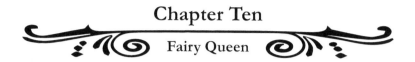

Fairy Queen

The swarm of fairies herded us deeper into the woods.

Ruburt's eyes shifted from the fairies to me. "Don't talk to 'em, and don't touch 'em, unless you want to be tainted with their fairy magic," he whispered under his breath.

I nodded and watched the fairies float around us like unshackled stars. How could such beautiful creatures be dangerous?

The flowers and trees sparkled with fine, iridescent dust.

More fairies gathered along the trail to watch as the army paraded Ruburt, Cassi, and I toward the heart of the fairy kingdom.

Both young and old peered at us with amused and curious expressions. One small fairy smiled and waved at me. I waved back.

Ruburt let out a horrified gasp. "Don't do that. Don't encourage 'em."

I gave him a teasing glance. "Don't be frightened, Ruburt. The fairies don't bite."

"Yes, they do, and so do pixies." Cassi grinned, showing all her tiny teeth.

The trees shifted from behind, closing us in a tight cocoon. The complex web of interlaced branches shut out earthly light, but a shining tree stood like a majestic sun in the center of the fairy galaxy. Crystal pears adorned the tree of light, garnishing the boughs like jeweled teardrops. Strands of white vines hung like spun silk and glowed brighter than moonlight.

Drawn to the light, I shuffled through the iridescent fairy dust that carpeted the ground.

Ruburt grasped my arm and pointed to the transparent spheres of soft light rotating around the kingdom like a thousand planets in a universe. I steadied myself and watched the lights glide methodically around the gravitational pull of the flawless white tree. The shimmering dust seemed to pulse, making the kingdom appear to inhale and exhale with life.

Fairies peered from their nests in the treetops or from their homes carved out of velvety mushrooms. They whispered to each other and pointed toward Ruburt and me. Hundreds more fluttered overhead like bees in a hive, creating a constant shower of dust.

In the great white tree, one fairy stood out above the others. Cassi flew to me and whispered in my ear, "There be Anthea, queen of all fairies, pixies, and sprites."

My mouth went dry. "Qu . . . Queen?" I was in the presence of royalty. I never thought I would ever meet a queen, let alone one with magic.

Queen Anthea held herself with grace and nobility. She looked different from Cassi in many ways. The queen stood five times taller than the pixie. Her wings were large and colorful, like a jeweled butterfly. Cassi's

wings were slender and transparent, like a dragonfly's.

Queen Anthea's shimmering silver hair cascaded in waves around her young, but wise, face. "Why are you in our forest?" Though her voice radiated tranquility, Anthea looked at Ruburt and me with a stern gaze.

"We be on journey," Cassi explained with inappropriate playful exuberance.

The queen tilted her head and asked Cassi, "Why are you helping a dwarf?" Her tone indicated an ancient rivalry between the dwarves and fairies.

Ruburt smiled like a cornered fox. He froze like a statue and swallowed hard.

"He be protector," Cassi explained. Ruburt and I nodded in the background. Maybe it was best to have Cassi talk to the fairies. She knew their ways and laws.

"How do we know he is a protector?"

"See my weapon," Ruburt broke in and flashed his dagger.

I pushed Ruburt's arm down. "I thought you said 'don't talk to them.'"

The queen eyed me and lowered her golden scepter. "Young lady, what is your name?"

I immediately regretted drawing attention to myself. "Auriella," I answered in a small voice.

The fairies of the court gasped, and glitter poured around us. I wrung my hands together. Why were the fairies startled when they heard my name?

The queen raised her scepter, and the fairy chatter fell silent. Queen Anthea glanced around the kingdom and announced, "She is the one the Shadow Legion hunts."

I knew this announcement meant trouble. I stepped away and shook

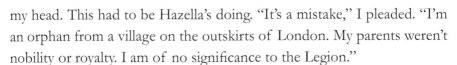

my head. This had to be Hazella's doing. "It's a mistake," I pleaded. "I'm an orphan from a village on the outskirts of London. My parents weren't nobility or royalty. I am of no significance to the Legion."

"You are Neviahan," the queen said without hesitation.

I put my fingertips to my lips. The blood drained from my face. Sweat dewed on my neck, and my hands stiffened like ice.

Ruburt slapped his hand over his brow. "I've been travelin' through a rebel-infested forest with the Legion's target?" He sounded more alarmed than angry. "That's like walkin' through a wolves' den with a deer carcass."

The air escaped my lungs in a single burst. I was the one in shock now. How could I be a Neviahan? Neviahans were strong, courageous, confident, celestial beings. I was just a weak, beaten orphan.

"The Shadow Legion believes you are the missing Lady of Neviah," the queen answered.

Ruburt dropped his shoulders and looked at me like he'd never seen me before. "The Lady of Neviah?" His voice held reverence and awe.

I crossed my arms under my chest. "Neviahans are great warriors. I am not. There is no way I can be the missing Lady of Neviah. I'm only fourteen." I turned to Ruburt and pleaded, "We need to explain to the fairies and the Legion that I'm not who they're looking for."

Ruburt stroked his beard as he assessed me.

Was level-headed Ruburt buying into this nonsense? Couldn't he see the tangled hair and filthy ragged clothes? I casually turned my leg to show the ugly scar from the Shadow Wolf. I thought for sure Ruburt would be my ally and explain to the fairies their dreadful error.

"It's not how you look, Auriella," Ruburt said in a fatherly tone. "It's how much you've survived. You're still alive." Ruburt's eyes flickered with hope. He grinned and shook his finger at me. "I knew it. I knew there was

something special 'bout you."

I clenched my cloak under my chin and assured, "I'm not the Lady of Neviah. There's nothing special about me." I sounded unsure, even to myself. If I wasn't a witch or demon, being a Neviahan was the only explanation for my power. This would definitely disrupt my plans for living a normal life, especially if my disastrous fiery flaws divulged themselves. If anyone else knew I was the Rebellion's target, they would shun me. I was doomed to live the rest of my life as a hermit—like Hazella. My teeth snapped together. "Is there a way we can know for sure?"

"There is only one way to know for sure." Anthea gripped her scepter. "Woldor the Wise is a historian of the Kingdom of Neviah. He will confirm whether you are the Lady of Neviah or not."

"Where do we find Woldor?" Ruburt asked.

"You can summon him at the Neviahan stone circle outside of Oswestry," the queen informed us.

Ruburt turned to me. "That's less than a day's journey." Excitement laced his voice. "I need to know," Ruburt whispered. "Thousands of people have waited for you . . ." Ruburt put his hands up and corrected, "I mean they have been waiting for the Lady of Neviah. If you are the Lady of Neviah, you carry a power that can save the human race from a demon holocaust."

I gulped. I wasn't about to tell Ruburt I could create fire. Besides, how could a plain old campfire help save the world from a holocaust?

"Lady Auriella," Queen Anthea addressed me, "you will need this ring." The queen motioned toward several fairies fluttering toward me with a brilliant ring.

I held out my palm. The cool metal of the ring hit my warm hand. Eight bright-colored gems lined the silver band and glistened in the light. I met the queen's eyes. "Why me?" I asked. I felt terrible that the queen

was giving me something so valuable out of false hope I was someone I wasn't.

The queen paused before she started to explain. "The correct question is 'Why not me?' Whether you are human, Neviahan, or the Lady of Neviah herself, you have the power to change this world. The world is at war with enemies they cannot see, monsters that blend with the shadows and disguise themselves as humans. The only way we can win this war is for everyone to do their part toward a single goal—peace. The victory over Erebus and the Shadow Legion is not about one man or woman doing a million great tasks, but about millions of people doing what they can."

I slid the bright ring on my finger. The sun sparkled off the spectrum of gems.

"This rainbow ring will protect you in the fairy borders. Once you are beyond our kingdom, let it remind you that, just like the rainbow, you are from the skies."

I touched the band on my finger and took a deep breath. I hoped that whatever Woldor said, Ruburt and the fairy queen wouldn't be disappointed if I wasn't who they hoped I was.

"Since you have chosen a dwarf to be your protector, he will need a proper weapon," Queen Anthea said.

"Whoa!" Ruburt shouted. He glanced down at his side and pulled a brilliant new dagger from the scabbard. Three white stones glowed like moons in the gold handle of the blade. The smooth blade glinted in the light of the fairy kingdom. "This is incredible. Is it magic?" Ruburt asked eagerly.

Queen Anthea pursed her lips. "We wouldn't want to give you something we've tainted with our fairy magic, now would we?"

Ruburt tightened his jaw and slid the dagger back in his scabbard.

Anthea continued, "We have something else that will help you on your journey."

A neigh came from behind us. Ruburt and I whirled around.

A flock a fairies led a butterscotch pony toward Ruburt.

"For me?" Ruburt gasped and took the reins.

Anthea grinned and leaned her weight against her scepter. "This is so you can keep up with Auriella. We know how slow old dwarves can be."

Ruburt grunted at the insult, but held his tongue.

"For Cassi, we have a fairy wand of power."

Cassi danced in a circle. She clutched a silver wand in her hand that spouted a streamer of white sparks.

Queen Anthea nodded toward the wand. "This wand will enhance the power you already have."

I imagined Ruburt's beard being twice as curly as Cassi had made it before. I put my hand to my mouth to suppress my giggle.

"Now, make haste to the Neviahan Circle. Call Woldor the Wise at the altar and don't stop for anything. You are being tracked."

Chapter Eleven

Shadow Wolves

The afternoon rain drizzled over me as I navigated the slippery path out of Clun Forest. Large drops of cold water flowed off the leaves overhead and splashed onto my face. I pulled the hood of my cloak tighter around my face. My warm breath hit the crisp air and rose in white puffs.

Ruburt's pony trotted beside me through the wet foliage. The horse relieved us of carrying the extra weight of the coins and supplies.

"What are you going to name your new horse?" I asked.

"I donno," Ruburt answered.

Cassi peered out from Ruburt's beard and asked, "How about Ruburt the Second?"

Ruburt's breath came out in a gust. "No, Cassi. We're not naming a female horse after me."

"But, she's so pretty," Cassi begged.

"You and your pixie ways have caused me enough trouble. Now be quiet or you can't ride in my beard anymore."

"But it's raining, and Cassi can't fly when wet." Cassi shivered, and

Ruburt's beard shook.

"Then I'll make you walk," Ruburt said.

"Cassi might walk into a spider's web, then what would we do? What would we do?"

"Enjoy the peace and quiet," Ruburt grunted.

I didn't blame Cassi for being afraid of spiders, especially after seeing her friend, Morning Dew, eaten by spiders. "What about naming the horse Morning Dew?" I asked.

"Morning Dew?" Ruburt mused and looked uncertain.

"Yes!" Cassi cheered.

Ruburt pinched his bushy eyebrows together. "I suppose it's better than Ruburt the Second."

We walked in silence, soaking wet, hungry, and tired. I tried to think of something else to distract my thoughts from the things the queen had said. If I, a fourteen-year-old girl, was the Lady of Neviah, then the world was in deep trouble. I couldn't handle a weapon, let alone fight off the entire Shadow Legion. I didn't know what would be worse, if my fiery abilities meant I was the Lady of Neviah or if they meant I was witch like Hazella.

The tree line of the great forest stopped, and Ruburt halted the horse. His deep voice interrupted my thoughts, "This is the edge of the Fairy Kingdom."

I scanned the fog-shrouded valley of wet foliage.

Ruburt pointed. "See the hill to the west? That's where we need to go."

I looked to where he pointed. A hill rose from the misty valley above the fog. A circle of stones crowned the top of the hill, and I could barely make out the altar where I would summon Woldor, the historian of Neviah. Mist from the storm covered the pathway between me and

my answer. Anything could be lurking in the dense fog the rain and cold created.

The glistening gems of the rainbow ring chimed like bells when the rain splashed onto my hand. "The ring won't protect me outside the forest," I remembered. "What should we do if we meet the Shadow Legion?" I tried to keep my voice steady so Ruburt wouldn't know I was scared.

The color drained from his face as he searched for an answer. His eyes fixed on the distant stone circle. "You must run."

"Run?" I repeated.

"I'll hold 'em off until you get to the Neviahan Circle and call Woldor the Wise."

"No." I gasped. "They'll kill you." How could Ruburt think I would run away and leave him to the Rebellion?

"It's you they want," he argued.

"That's why I should stay and you should run."

Ruburt shook his head. "Auriella, I know what the Shadow Legion can do: horrible, torturous, no regard for humanity." He paused from his sputtering. "Learn 'bout your powers so you can destroy 'em. You must stop 'em."

What was he talking about? I couldn't stop anything, let alone an adversary like a member of the Shadow Legion. "Ruburt, please don't sacrifice your life for me. I'm not the Lady of Neviah."

Ruburt's eyes met mine. Despite the situation, he smiled calmly. "I believe you are." There was no hint of sarcasm in his tone. "I'll ride alongside you, but if you hear or see anything unusual, keep running. Don't lose sight of the stone circle."

A knot tightened in my throat. I blinked back the hot tears of terror before nodding.

"Now, run!" Ruburt commanded and kicked the sides of his pony.

I took off at a sprint through the rain-soaked valley. The pony's hooves sloshed through the muddy foliage beside me.

The fog blinded me from anything more than a few paces ahead. I could no longer see the Neviahan Circle past the cloud bank. Dread washed over me. What if I was going the wrong way? What if I was racing toward a trap?

I plunged forward into a pond I didn't see through the fog. The cold water hit me like shards of ice penetrating my skin. Ruburt halted his pony as I regained my footing and waded back to the bank.

"We can't stop." Ruburt's eyes darted around, trying to see through the fog.

"We have to somehow go around this pond," I said and wrung out my cloak and nightgown.

Ruburt shook his head. "No, you have to swim across."

"What?" I said. "No!"

"We know this is the path to the Neviahan Circle. If we veer from the straight course we may miss it completely. It's too deep for my pony to swim across. I have to take the long way around."

I planted my feet on the bank. "I'm not leaving you."

I hardly got the sentence out before a ghostly howl echoed through the pounding rain. Lightning whipped overhead.

"Go!" Ruburt shouted. "I'll lead them away." He kicked the sides of his pony and galloped off.

My heart pounded inside my chest like an executioner's drum. The sound of my breath rushed in and out. I plunged into the water. My arms swung overhead and paddled against the frigid pond. My legs tangled in my cloak and held me back. I reached for the ties and unfastened the

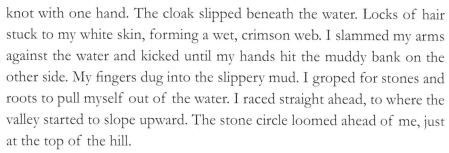

knot with one hand. The cloak slipped beneath the water. Locks of hair stuck to my white skin, forming a wet, crimson web. I slammed my arms against the water and kicked until my hands hit the muddy bank on the other side. My fingers dug into the slippery mud. I groped for stones and roots to pull myself out of the water. I raced straight ahead, to where the valley started to slope upward. The stone circle loomed ahead of me, just at the top of the hill.

The bellow of a wolf resonated from the east, then another from the west. The echo of their haunting voices flooded the valley. Lightning flashed overhead and thunder shook the earth.

I fought my way through the wet foliage and squinted my eyes to pierce the fog. Leaves slapped against my skin and clothes. My foot struck a slick, mossy stone, and I heard a sharp crack as I plummeted to the ground. Pain shot from my ankle to my knee.

Stifling a scream, I clawed at the earth and scrambled to my feet. I tried to walk, but my leg gave out. I clenched my teeth and grabbed my ankle. It seemed all the forces of nature were working against me.

Just when I thought it couldn't get any worse, a dark spirit in a shadowy human form, stepped from the shroud of fog and glided toward me. I covered my mouth to quiet my rapid breathing. The shadowy human form crouched down on all fours and transformed. Matted fur sprang from its back. Its eyes flashed like brimstone. It stretched out a massive paw and took another step toward me. "She's close. I can smell her blood," the wolf said.

Two other wolves stepped from the fog and followed the alpha wolf as they searched for me. Their gums flailed hideously over their jagged teeth as they took in my scent. They moved toward me, their ears pulled back as they prowled near.

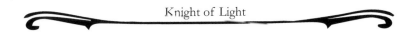

I lay low in the brush. Each thud of my heart was like a mallet pounding a stake, fastening me to the ground until I couldn't move at all.

The pack strode toward me. The wolves' large claws hit against the stones. Even if I could have moved, there was nowhere to run.

Lightning struck a nearby tree. Deadly screams from a whip of lightning echoed in the night. The tree crashed to the earth, its mighty branches snapped like twigs. The ground shook, making the pebbles at my feet bounce.

The piercing gaze of the alpha wolf met mine and flashed with hunger.

"No," I stammered and held up my hand uselessly. The wolves bounded forward in unison. My eyes snapped shut, and my body curled in a ball.

"Go, Auriella!" Ruburt shouted. He and his pony appeared out of the mist. The small, golden animal reared up, momentarily blocking the wolves' path.

There was no way that Ruburt was going to be able to defend himself against three Shadow Wolves. I clenched my fists, unbound my curled body and leaped up. I ignored all my pain as conviction filled my heart, and fire burst from my hands and up my arms like torches. Hot golden flames enveloped my body. I took a stance and tossed an erratic stream of fire in the wolves' direction.

Ruburt fell from his horse and covered his eyes to protect them from the blinding burst of energy.

The inferno consumed the alpha wolf. The shadow of a man emerged from the wolf's carcass, screamed, and clawed at his featureless face as he disintegrated into ash.

Fire whirled around me in streams of sparkling, gold waves. The

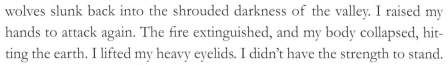
wolves slunk back into the shrouded darkness of the valley. I raised my hands to attack again. The fire extinguished, and my body collapsed, hitting the earth. I lifted my heavy eyelids. I didn't have the strength to stand.

Ruburt crawled toward me. "Auriella?" his voice sounded terrified. "Auriella, say something!"

Cassi, who had been hiding in Ruburt's beard, whimpered and pulled at her dark curls.

I peered through my eyelashes, but couldn't speak.

Ruburt whirled around and pulled his dagger from the scabbard. "Stay away," he shouted.

A wolf stepped toward us. "Now, we know," the wolf said in a low growl. "We've seen it with our own eyes. We will be back with weapons and an army."

Ruburt lunged forward with his dagger extended, splitting the wolf's nose. Dark blood dripped from the muzzle of the beast. The wolf snapped at Ruburt, slammed his massive paw on the dwarf, and pinned him to the ground. Ruburt's dagger flew from his hand and bounced toward the pond.

"Ho! Who goes there?" A voice shouted. The ground quaked under me. I fought to find the strength to move.

"We'll return for the prize," the wolf promised and fled into the fog.

Three riders on horseback broke through the fog and pulled up on their reins. The horses stirred and stomped their hooves against the ground.

"What's going on?" one of the men asked. "We heard an explosion."

"I . . . I . . ." Ruburt stammered. "We were attacked by Shadow Wolves."

"Shadow Wolves?" the man questioned.

"Yes, those beastly monsters you villagers call Black Shucks or Moddey Dhoo."

"Look, it's a lady." The one who spoke, the youngest of the riders, jumped from his horse and rushed toward me.

"Is she alive, Alwaien?" A young man with dark hair and tanned skin asked a third man.

Alwaien dismounted and leaned over me. "I don't know. Fredrick, come look at her."

I desperately wished I had the strength to speak.

Fredrick jumped effortlessly from his horse. All three young men leaned over me. Fredrick put his head to my chest. "She has a heartbeat. Quick, help me get her on the horse."

"She's so beautiful," the youngest of the three said. "It's like she's not even human."

Chapter Twelve

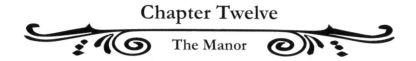

The Manor

I blinked, as if trying to shed blurry scales from my eyes and assessed the mysterious room. It was twice the size of Hazella's cottage, and all four walls were made of warm gray stone. Curtains the color of sunflowers hung from several windows and wrapped around the poles rising from the head and foot of the bed I lay on. The bright room smelled as fresh as a spring morning.

"Auriella, you're awake!" Ruburt's gentle voice echoed relief.

"Where am I?" I brushed the heavy quilt with my fingertips and tried to rise and examine the room.

Ruburt lifted his hands, stopping me. "You are in Oswestry."

My heart beat fiercely. The embarrassing début of being a barefooted, ragged, orphan in the new village was over—I'd slept through the whole thing. I lifted the covers and peered under. At least my ragged nightgown still covered my naked body. What a relief.

Dizziness overcame me, and I lay on the white downy pillows, forcing

my eyes to stay open as I examined the splendid room of sunshine.

Cassi poked her head out of Ruburt's beard and exclaimed, "Cassi so happy to see Auriella!"

"You stay hidden, Cassi," Ruburt commanded in a fatherly tone, "unless you want to end up in a cage again."

"How did I get here?" I asked.

"Lady Hannah's sons heard the wolves and rescued us. Lady Hannah gave us both rooms to stay in while you recover, but we'll need to move on quickly. Two wolves got away. As soon as they return to the Legion and report our whereabouts, this place will be swarming with rebels."

I sat up. "Will the people here be in danger? I don't want someone hurt because of me."

"It doesn't matter," Ruburt said. "We need to make sure you're safe before the Legion invades."

This was all my fault. People could be killed because of me. "But—"

The door to my room snapped opened.

My heart leaped in my chest, I clenched my teeth and gripped my blankets. Ruburt put his hand over his dagger.

A woman entered, carrying a bowl of hot soup. Her step was lively. Neatly combed blonde hair framed her fair, clean face. Her dress smelled like lavender, and her shoes were polished to a shine. Even her teeth and fingernails were pristine. I never imagined a person could look so heavenly.

"Good morning. My name is Leah. I am Lady Hannah's nurse."

Leah brushed back my hair and placed a soft hand on my forehead. "You are still too warm. It's like you have been on fire."

I bit my lip—if they only knew.

"Lady Hannah asked me to make sure you are cared for. Is it all right if I see where you are hurt?"

I hesitated. There would be too many uncomfortable questions if Leah saw the scars on my back. To my relief, she pointed to my ankle. I lifted my ankle and nodded my consent. I noticed something about Leah I had not seen in any other human—her smile. Her smile could light a room and make any winter warm.

Leah unwrapped the bandage that had been tied around my ankle. "Your ankle is not broken, but you shouldn't run or jump until next week."

Leah rebound my ankle, then paused, asking gently, "How did you get the marks on your back?"

My fingers sank into the quilt, gripping it tightly. They must have noticed my back while I was passed out. How do you explain that a crazy, old witch captured you and tortured you to find out your power so she would know how valuable of a bargaining chip you were in negotiations with the Shadow Legion? If the people of this village knew about my power, would they do the same? Or would they also think I was a witch and try to boil me alive?

Leah lifted my chin. "It's all right. No one here is going to hurt you. It must have happened a long time ago. The marks have healed well."

Every time I used my power, it seemed to heal my flesh. I squinted at my ankle. Apparently, the healing fire didn't work on internal injuries.

"Lady Hannah wants to see you when you are stronger and can get around easier. I will return later this evening with dinner and to see if your fever has broken." Leah curtsied and closed the door behind her as she left.

"Wow, she is so lovely," I said in amazement.

"That's what I thought, too." Ruburt chuckled, and his cheeks grew bright.

"I hope there are more people like her in this village." I looked at

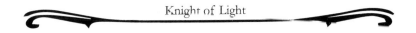

my generous portion of pea soup, and slowly brought a spoonful of the savory soup to my mouth. Just the smell made me feel better, and the taste was divine.

While the soup was a wonderful start, it took a few more days before I recovered from my weakened condition. Leah visited me often, and each time she brought larger portions of food. One day, Leah brought beef stew with potatoes and a roll smothered in butter. Leah sat with me as I ate.

"Are there many people in this village?" I asked her.

"Yes, this is one of the largest towns united under the English flag," Leah answered. "Lady Hannah has a son who is fifteen. He planned to wait a few years before he started looking for a wife, but after he saw you, he's reconsidering his decision."

I cringed. How could anyone find me appealing in this condition? The son of nobility, no matter how undesirable in appearance or manner, would have better prospects than a beaten orphan girl.

"I'm sorry," Leah gasped. "You must already be betrothed?"

"No, I'm not." My cheeks burned with embarrassment. "But I'm only fourteen." I took deep breaths to calm my nerves so the fire wouldn't combust from my fingers.

"I see," Leah sounded disappointed. "Then we must return you to your parents."

"I don't have any parents." I shook my head. "They died when I was young."

"You poor thing." Leah doted over me and patted my hand. "Feel free to make yourself at home until your meeting with Lady Hannah. She will help you get to where you need to go. You seem well enough to walk, and getting out of this cramped room will do you some good."

Cramped? My room was massive! If Leah thought this was tight quarters, what did the rest of the manor look like?

I took Leah's suggestion and explored the manor that afternoon. Burning torches, intricate tapestries, and portraits hung on the labyrinth hallways of stone. I turned a corner and followed the sound of excited voices chattering. The aroma of food mixed with other unknown scents tantalized my senses.

I followed the smells and sounds to a large room. The room had a massive fireplace with a huge glazed roast turning above the flames. Many women, busy as bees, prepared food on long wooden tables. They wore their hair in tight buns and crisp aprons covered their long skirts. The sleeves on their billowing shirts were scrunched to their elbows. I had never seen so many people in one place before, but somehow the room looked organized as they all worked together.

One of the women glanced at me and gasped. "Oh girls! Look who has come to join us." They rushed toward me at once like a stampede.

I retreated against the wall.

"Do not be afraid, dearie. We won't hurt you," a cook said.

I searched their plump, beaming faces. They were excited, but not angry. Their smiles were warm and genuine, not malicious like Hazella's when she was scheming.

A woman took my hand and led me into the kitchen. "Well, just look at this beautiful young lady. Have you ever seen anything more precious in your life?"

"Or so dirty?" another woman added and wrinkled her nose.

They fussed over my appearance, saying to each other:

"Look at that tangled hair and those tattered clothes."

"Such dirty feet!"

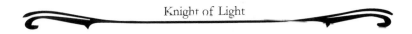

"What a gorgeous face."

"There's something unusual about her," one of them added, suspiciously.

I held my breath. What if they noticed something alien about me . . . something not human?

"Look at her snowy white skin and flaming red hair. Her soft, innocent beauty seems too . . . exotic."

They all eyed me.

The game was over. They weren't going to buy that I was human.

"Do you think she's from Ireland?"

"Nonsense," the head cook cut in. "Just because she's filthy, doesn't mean she's a barbarian. We need to get her a good hot bath. Oh, and we better take her to the seamstress to get her some new clothes to wear. Jacquine has wanted to make some clothes for a young lady for as long as I can remember. This might be her only chance since Lady Hannah only has sons."

The women giggled in chorus.

A few of them whisked me out of the warm kitchen and marched me up a flight of stairs. One of the cooks opened the door and called out, "Oh, Jacquine, look what we have found!"

Jacquine stopped her sewing when I entered the room. Jacquine was as beautiful as the fairy queen. She wore her wavy black hair in a loose bun. She was not as heavy as the cooks, but much taller.

"Oh my!" Jacquine gasped in delight and approached me with her hands clasped. "Well, aren't you a pretty thing?" A few wrinkles appeared around her eyes when she smiled.

I lowered my head to let my hair cover my face. My cheeks grew hot.

"We were hoping you could make Auriella something suitable to

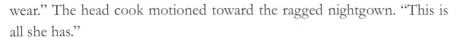

wear." The head cook motioned toward the ragged nightgown. "This is all she has."

"Oh!" Shame rang in Jacquine's voice. "We can't have her wearing that." Jacquine opened one chest after another, before opening the closet doors. Cloth of every imaginable color filled each chest and shelf. The stunning colors combined with the light from the stained glass window, sending a kaleidoscope of rainbows dancing through the room. "Which color would you like?" Jacquine asked.

I stood in awe, looking around the rainbow room. One color stood out from all the others. I pointed to the color I thought most represented freedom and my new life in Oswestry. It was the color of a clear, summer sky.

"Oh, the lass likes blue," one of the cooks cooed.

Jacquine proceeded to pull numerous other colors of fabric out of the closets and placed them with the blue cloth in a pile on her sewing bench. "Let me get your measurements now, dearie."

Jacquine wrapped the string around my waist. "Oh my, look how skinny you are!"

The cooks wagged their heads.

The head cook held up a finger. "Apple cobbler?"

"That's just what she needs," Jacquine agreed.

The cooks rushed down the hall, chattering about fancy foods that would fatten me up.

Was Jacquine really going to make me new clothes? "I'm not anyone important," I politely reminded. "I can make do." I had never worn a new dress before and felt guilty at the thought of owning such a thing.

Jacquine started measuring my arm length and shoulder width. "No, dear, you are not dressing like a homeless orphan child."

I swallowed too quickly and coughed.

"Oh goodness," Jacquine stopped measuring. "Don't tell me you are an orphan."

I nodded.

"It's a good thing you found your way here." Jacquine continued to measure. "Until you find a place to stay, all of us will look after you."

Jacquine marked the string with several straight pins and finished her measuring. "There now, we must get you cleaned before you get into your new clothes."

Clean. I couldn't wait. After everything I'd been through, washing my hands and face would help me feel human again. I sighed at that thought, knowing it wasn't completely accurate. The only thing that would truly help me feel human again would be to meet with Woldor, the Neviahan historian. He would settle the misunderstanding, or at least help me stop my internal inferno so I could be normal.

Chapter Thirteen

Boiled Alive

Jacquine took me down a long flight of stairs, until we came to a doorway with steam billowing between the cracks. We entered, and Jacquine called out, "Maryweather!"

Out of the warm mist stepped a large woman with a round face and big, brown eyes. A cloth was wrapped around her head and covered her hair. Her expression was stern, but somehow, her apple cheeks made it seem like she was smiling.

"Maryweather, this is Auriella. She has come to stay with us. I am making the lass some new clothes, but, before I will let her wear them, she needs to be clean."

Maryweather put her hands on her hefty hips and looked at me, shaking her head. "Well, we'll have ta find a way ta scrub all that dirt off her face."

"I will leave her in your care so I can begin my sewing." Jacquine turned and left me alone with this new stranger.

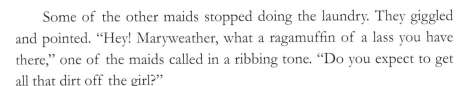

Some of the other maids stopped doing the laundry. They giggled and pointed. "Hey! Maryweather, what a ragamuffin of a lass you have there," one of the maids called in a ribbing tone. "Do you expect to get all that dirt off the girl?"

"I don't think she has ever had a bath in her life!" another put in.

"We better get ta work. It's gonna take some hard scrubbin' ta get all the filth off you before dinner." Maryweather scrutinized me with critical eyes. She didn't dote over me like everyone else had. It was as if she could see into my soul and pull out my secrets. Perhaps she already knew I was a fraud. I couldn't fool everyone.

Taking me by the hand, Maryweather led me behind a thin curtain to a small pool of water. It was the perfect place to try and drown me to see if I was a witch. Steam rose from the water and bubbles floated across the surface. Bubbles in water meant it was scalding hot.

"Get in," Maryweather commanded, as if I didn't have a choice.

It was true. She thought I was a witch and wanted to boil me! Someone from my old village must have recognized me and told her about my power. I recoiled toward the exit.

Maryweather's firm grip clenched onto my wrist. I tried to pull away, but Maryweather held on tighter. "I don't think so." Maryweather's face turned red. "You're not leaving now."

"No!" I screamed. "I'm human! You're making a mistake." I turned and bolted for the door. I tried to create my fire so I could protect myself, but nothing came. What a time for my power to leave. Maybe I used up the last of the fire when I fought the wolves.

Two laundry maids blocked the door. I tried to shove past them to the stairwell.

"She's savage," one of them gasped.

What were they talking about? I wasn't savage. I just wanted to live.

Maryweather grabbed hold of my arm and dragged me toward the hot water.

I screamed. My voice came out high-pitched and panicky. I fought to free myself from the massive woman's grip.

Maryweather called, "Emilie, Doris, Eliza, I need your help!"

Three more women jumped me from behind. Each grabbed a leg or arm and held on.

"I'm not a witch!" I howled and kicked. They carried me to the pool and tossed me in, clothes and all. I fought for my life as I sank to the bottom. Crystal-blue water swirled around me as I struggled toward the surface. I swallowed some water and resisted the urge to gasp, realizing I would just inhale more liquid. In the water, I was more vulnerable than in the jaws of a wolf. There was no light, no air, and no ability to heal or protect myself with fire.

The pool was only three feet deep, but I seemed to sink forever before I felt the bottom and stood erect. I sprang to the surface, coughing and gasping for breath. I slapped against the warm water and fought to get to the edge.

"Ladies, do not let her out of the water!"

They surrounded the pool, and every time I came close to the edge, they pushed me into the middle.

"This will never do!" Emilie shook her head. "She will never get clean this way. Here, let me get into the pool with the poor lass and show her how to clean herself." Emilie took off her overdress and got in with me.

I stopped fighting and watched Emilie wade into the water. I popped a bubble floating across the surface. "It's soap," I realized out loud. They weren't trying to kill me. My body adjusted to the warm water, and the

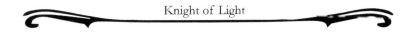
heat actually felt nice.

"Yes, it's soap. And you're going to need lots of it," Maryweather said. "Haven't you ever bathed before?" From the side of the pool, she tossed Emilie a bar of soap.

"Of course I have! I just haven't taken a swim while washing before," I trailed off, feeling foolish as the women laughed in an uproar.

Emilie smiled and lifted the cream-colored bar. "Now, I don't know what savage raised you, but you need to learn to clean yourself. Watch me clean myself with this soap." She rubbed it on her arm, creating a lather of white bubbles, then slipped her arm into the pool and rinsed it off. The lather dissolved and she brought her arm out of the water. I couldn't see any difference between Emilie's clean arm and her dirty arm.

"Now lass, you're not going to get out of this pool of water until you're clean." Emilie's voice held a stiff warning. She dropped the bar of soap in my palm.

I narrowed my eyes and scrubbed at my arm. Of course I would show them I could clean myself. This was no different than cleaning Hazella's pots, but, unlike the pots, I wasn't Hazella's property anymore, and I didn't want any of Hazella's dirt on me. I scrubbed harder, as if trying to scrub bad memories of Hazella away.

Dirty, brown lather foamed under the bar of soap on my skin. I slid my arm into the pool and scrubbed some more. I pulled my arm out of the water and stared at my skin. Stripped of the dirt, my left arm glowed like pure ivory.

The maids on the side of the pool let down their guard. They looked relieved and not as vicious as they had before. Even Emilie looked more relaxed, "Now, off with your clothes so you can clean your whole body."

I peeled off my old nightgown and handed it to one of the maids.

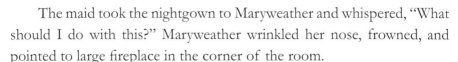

The maid took the nightgown to Maryweather and whispered, "What should I do with this?" Maryweather wrinkled her nose, frowned, and pointed to large fireplace in the corner of the room.

I rubbed myself with the bar of soap many times, as streams of muddy water trickled off me. Emilie helped me clean my feet. I jerked away, giggled, then slipped under the water and allowed myself to float. It almost felt like flying through warm clouds and soft wind. Fully immersed, I felt like I was washing away the old me who was filthy, uneducated, and afraid, then resurfacing a clean, bright lady who could take on the world.

Emilie interrupted my reverie. "You need to wash your hair now." I had never washed my hair like this before and didn't know what to do. Seeing my confusion, she said, "Come here and let me help you."

I waited while Emilie lathered my ravaged hair and rinsed it in the water. We washed my hair not only once, but a half a dozen times. "Oh, I will never ever get this hair untangled!" Emilie declared, "It is all matted into a knotted mess! We are going to need a comb and shears to make your hair look better."

"Cut my hair?" I asked. I forced myself to be calm. I'd overreacted too many times already. "All right," I agreed.

Maryweather handed towels to Emilie and me as we stepped out of the pool of water. Emilie retrieved some shears and a comb, then worked over my hair. Emilie pulled at my hair, trying to separate the locks with the comb. She had to cut out a lot of the tangles. I gritted my teeth every time Emilie pulled at my hair and each time a lock of red hair fell to the floor.

Emilie gasped and dropped her arms to her side. "Oh, no!"

"What is it?" I asked. Obviously, from Emilie's startled reaction, something was afoot. This couldn't be good.

It seemed like an eternal moment of wondering what abnormality

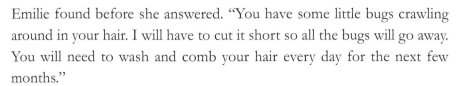

Emilie found before she answered. "You have some little bugs crawling around in your hair. I will have to cut it short so all the bugs will go away. You will need to wash and comb your hair every day for the next few months."

I hated Hazella's dirt on me. I was even more horrified that Hazella's bugs had made a nest of my hair.

After an hour of combing and cutting, Emilie finally finished. I looked like a new person. Only about two inches of curly hair remained on my head. My milky white skin contrasted the brownish dirt color that previously covered me.

The laundry maids draped a long nightgown over my thin, clean body. Emilie escorted me to my room. At the door, Emilie bid me a good evening before departing.

When I entered my bedroom, Ruburt and Cassi were there. They looked like they had been waiting for me. Ruburt smiled. "You look different."

"I know. I'm clean, and my fire curse is gone," I said, thinking about how I had used the last of it up on the wolves. "I really am human!" I drifted toward the glass window to see my reflection. The sunlight touched me. The colors of lavender, gold, jade, and rose shimmered iridescently off my skin. I jerked my arm out of the light.

"What's wrong?" Cassi asked.

"Can you see this?" I pointed at my arm.

Ruburt came near and examined my arm. "I don't see anything."

I stepped into the sunlight streaking through the window. Light reflected off my arm and shimmered like the fairy kingdom.

"I don't see what you're talking about." Ruburt lifted one eyebrow. Cassi shrugged her shoulders.

"I look like an overgrown fairy!" I couldn't live in Oswestry like this. Everyone would know something was wrong with me. I put my hand to my forehead. I was doomed to life as a hermit—like Hazella.

Ruburt pulled a small inspecting glass from his goldsmith bag and held it to my skin. I rolled my eyes. Was he just trying to make me feel better?

"Your skin is glistening. It looks like you're made of opals."

I pulled my arm away and dropped onto my bed. "What is wrong with me?"

"I wouldn't worry about it. No one is going to notice unless they get close to you in the sunlight."

The door flew open. Cassi dove into Ruburt's beard. Three cooks entered the room, carrying a large tray of apple cobbler. Four maids followed the cooks, and they smiled and curtsied when they entered. The charade was over and I was in trouble. They were bound to notice me, sparkling like an opal fairy now that I'd scrubbed all the dirt off.

One of the cooks set the cobbler on the table next to my bed. "Just look at her!"

I clenched my nightgown in my fists and tightened my jaw.

"You can see the lass's face, now that all the dirt is gone."

"The lass is prettier than a bright red apple!" another cook commented.

While the cooks examined me, the four maids tore the old linens from my bed and replaced them, topping the bed with fresh new pillows and a warm quilt.

"Oh dearie, if you are still hungry after you have eaten this food, come to the kitchen, and we'll make you a snack."

The cooks and maids hadn't said anything yet about my appearance. Could they not see I was a monster?

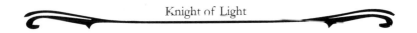

Ruburt gazed at the apple cobbler like there was nothing to worry about. Cassi peered out through Ruburt's beard where she hid and licked her lips.

"Thank you." I tried to curtsy like the maids had done. My legs shook awkwardly. Maybe Ruburt was right and I could get away with yet another abnormality. If the fire came back it would be easy to hide and if no one but me could see my strange skin, then I could be normal.

The cooks and maids curtsied in return and left us to enjoy dessert.

As soon as they were gone, Cassi flew full speed toward the food, spinning and flipping in somersaults through the air. "Cassi could eat a whole Skipobottomoss!" She grasped several handfuls of food and gobbled it in big bites.

"A Skipobottomoss?" Ruburt raised a skeptical eyebrow. "What in the world is a Skipo. . . ."

Cassi started to answer, but Ruburt shook his head to cut her off. "I don't want to know," he said, before he piled food onto his plate and started to eat.

I was hungry, too, but I couldn't quit looking at my skin.

"They didn't see it," I sighed in relief.

"See what?" Ruburt asked with a full mouth.

I shook my head. He was too preoccupied by the dessert.

"Nothing, I guess." Maybe I could fit in, and why not? After all, I was human.

Chapter Fourteen

Lady Hannah

My door swung open. "Good morning!" Jacquine sang out and pulled back the curtains. Blinding rays of sunlight flashed into the room. I tossed the blankets over my head. I wasn't used to this much light and had no idea if my skin was still acting strange.

"Come now, it's time to rise. Your clothes are finished."

I peered out from behind the quilt. Jacquine placed several dresses at the foot of the bed.

She put her hands on her hips and tilted her head as she eyed me. "Oh, I know what you're hiding."

She did? Did Jacquine know about my strange fairy-like skin?

"Don't worry, your hair will grow back soon enough." Jacquine lifted a pretty, blue dress. "Let me help you get dressed."

I lowered the blanket. Obviously, Jacquine couldn't see the abnormal skin either. I brushed my arm, then lifted my nightgown and stared at my glittering legs. Apparently, I was the only one who noticed this new change.

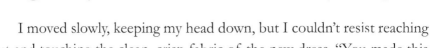

I moved slowly, keeping my head down, but I couldn't resist reaching out and touching the clean, crisp fabric of the new dress. "You made this for me?"

"Yes. All for you." Jacquine tossed the dress over my head and tightened the laces on the gown. I squirmed back and forth, trying to get used to the feel of clothes that actually fit.

"Now, a surprise." Jacquine held her hands behind her. "We had a cobbler make something special for you." Jacquine pulled a pair of brown leather slippers from behind her back. "What do you think?"

"Shoes!" I gasped. "I can't believe it. They're beautiful. Are you sure?" I reached for the dainty-looking slippers, but stepped away. "I can't."

"Just put them on," Jacquine insisted.

She set them on the floor by my feet. I hesitated before slipping them on. I wiggled my toes against the cushiony surface and felt like dancing and running. I couldn't help but giggle.

I stretched out my arms and spun around to show the entire ensemble, then threw my arms around Jacquine. "Thank you. This is the best gift anyone has ever given me."

Jacquine's eyes sparkled with tears. "Oh dearie, it was my pleasure." She stepped back to admire the dress on me. "It's perfect and just in time. Lady Hannah would like to meet you after breakfast."

I was excited, but nervous to meet Lady Hannah. I quickly ate then followed an escort down a long mahogany hallway to Lady Hannah's room.

When I entered Lady Hannah's chambers the escort shut the heavy polished door and the brass handle clicked behind her. I squinted to examine the intimidating, dim room. The windows were covered in dark navy curtains. The only light came from an oil lamp at Lady Hannah's bedside. The noblewoman sat in her bed with pillows propped behind her. Her

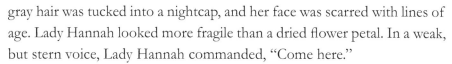

gray hair was tucked into a nightcap, and her face was scarred with lines of age. Lady Hannah looked more fragile than a dried flower petal. In a weak, but stern voice, Lady Hannah commanded, "Come here."

I stepped near the bed and smiled my prettiest smile.

Lady Hannah lifted a magnifying glass and examined me from head to toe. I froze in place. At least the curtains were drawn, blocking out the sunlight that would reveal my unusual skin under the magnifying glass. I stood tall and wondered if I should speak, curtsey, or try to do something to impress Lady Hannah.

Lady Hannah lowered the magnifying glass and said, "My sons informed me you were severely damaged, but you appear in good health."

"Yes, m'lady." I automatically curtsied. "Your staff has cared for me, and I want to repay you for the kindness."

Lady Hannah reached for her water goblet on the table next to the bed. "I assure you, that will not be necessary. But, we need to return you to where you belong. Someone must be worried about you. Are you from Oswestry?"

"No. I'm not from anywhere."

"Come now, that is not possible. Young women don't just fall out of the sky." Lady Hannah set the glass on the table and laced her hands together. "Have you a mother, a father, or any relatives?"

"No, I was orphaned years ago, and I now live on my own," I said. I felt a stinging in my eyes. I didn't want to cry about my past, especially not in front of the duchess. I had to quickly change the subject. I stammered, "But I have two friends. A dwarf named Ruburt and . . .." I stopped, remembering that Ruburt had told Cassi to stay hidden. People weren't supposed to know about her because they might try to take her magic dust. "Just Ruburt," I corrected.

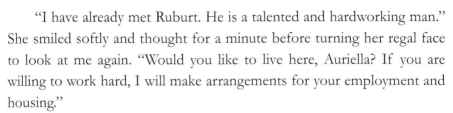

"I have already met Ruburt. He is a talented and hardworking man." She smiled softly and thought for a minute before turning her regal face to look at me again. "Would you like to live here, Auriella? If you are willing to work hard, I will make arrangements for your employment and housing."

"Oh! I would like that!" I restrained myself from bouncing around the room. I would have a real home. Hazella would never think to look for me in the manor.

"Well, that settles it." Lady Hannah clapped her hands three times, and three tall young men entered the room. I stepped against the wall. The boys stood like stately soldiers next to Lady Hannah's bed. She pointed to one of them. "This is Alwaien, Lord of Oswestry. He is my eldest son and master of the guards and manor affairs." She pointed toward the second young man. "This is Fredrick, my second son. He is the master of the farms and business affairs." She turned toward the third young man and continued, "And this is Lucas, my third son, master of the stables and livestock. My three sons manage the estate. You are to follow their instructions."

I swallowed hard and prayed they wouldn't be harsh taskmasters like Hazella. I met the eyes of the youngest master. The sandy-haired boy regally composed himself and looked away. I tightened my jaw and looked to his mother.

The elegant woman smiled at me, and I felt a strange sensation in my chest. It was warm and comforting, like somehow, I just knew everything would be all right. Lady Hannah continued, "You will be assigned to work with each of my sons. In the morning, you will work with Lucas at the stables. In the afternoon, you will work with Fredrick in the fields. In the evening, you will help Lord Alwaien's people in the kitchen. Come see me

on Saturday and Sunday to learn the skills of a lady-in-waiting."

Lady-in-waiting? I thought. Hazella always told me to hurry, but Lady Hannah was going to make me wait?

With their mother's closing statement, the gentlemen each bowed, presenting themselves to me and kissed the top of my hand. Lucas pecked my hand and dashed out the door like he had been shocked by my touch.

Fear and confusion surged through me. Did he know something was wrong with me? Why was I suddenly terrified of him, but at the same time, drawn to him?

Lady Hannah excused me from the room. I couldn't stop thinking about Master Lucas. I clasped my hands together and walked lithely to Ruburt's room and knocked on the door.

Ruburt opened the door a crack and peered out. He smiled when he saw me and opened the door wide. Several bags of supplies lay on his bed.

I scrunched my eyebrows together. "Are you going somewhere?"

"We both are." Ruburt said quickly. "Those Shadow Wolves know we are in Oswestry. We have to leave before they demolish the town."

My heart dropped. "Leave?" I couldn't leave now. For the first time in years, I actually had a chance to be a part of a family. It might be my only chance to have a normal life. I stood firmly in place. "I'm not leaving."

"But the Shadow Legion has seen you here." Ruburt stuffed a pair of socks in his bag.

"Yes, but look at me." I turned around and ran my fingers through my short hair. "I look different since they saw me."

Ruburt pressed his lips into a line and stopped packing.

I crossed my arms. "I am going to work for Lady Hannah."

Ruburt leaned against the bed. "Lady Hannah offered you a job too?"

I nodded and asked, "She offered you a job?"

"She asked me to be the manor blacksmith." He stroked his long beard like he was considering the idea of staying. "It would be good work, and Hazella would never think to look for me outside a dwarf village."

"Please." I clasped my hands in a pleading manner.

"It'll be dangerous," Ruburt cautioned. "Cassi will have to keep a look out and search the woods for any sign of the Shadow Legion. If she sees anything, we hide in the fairy forest." He pointed to my hand. "Do you still have the rainbow ring?"

I lifted my hand and shifted my fingers to make the gems glitter.

"Good," Ruburt said. "Keep it on you always. It's only a matter of time before the Rebellion finds us."

Chapter Fifteen

Master Lucas

I arose early, got dressed, and bounded for the stables, ready for my new employment. I would train with each of the dukes and learn everything there was to know about the manor. I pressed open the stable door. Master Lucas was nowhere in sight.

Large, majestic horses stared at me with big, dark eyes. They seemed just as curious about me as I was about them. I reached out to touch a horse's soft nose. The doors flew open and slammed against the walls. The whole stable quivered. The startled horses whinnied. I dove for a pile of straw in the corner.

Lucas jumped through the doors and swung a sword through the air. "Come on! Is that all you've got?" he asked in a taunting tone. The tall young man danced around the stables and waved his sword. Stray strands of sandy hair escaped his ponytail and curled around his face, which sported a scruff of facial hair on his chin and upper lip. His arms were thin, but toned from years of hard work in the stables.

He spun, gave a dramatic final jab with his sword and called in triumph, "Gotcha! You will think twice before challenging Sir Lucas again!" I clapped my hands, applauding Lucas's victory over his imaginary foe. Lucas faced me, his eyes wide. The momentary look of surprise melted and a curious grin spread across his face. He graciously bowed to me, his one-woman audience. The show energized me, and I desperately wanted to learn to do what Lucas had just done.

"I'm impressed." I straightened out my skirt and giggled.

"Well," Lucas lowered his voice, smiled warmly, and stroked his chin. "It was nothing, really." He tucked his sword into his belt and held out his hand to help me rise. "Let us get on with the chores. There's a lot of work to do." His light blue eyes twinkled at me genuinely as he winked. Working with Lucas was going to be fun.

Lucas and I fed and watered the horses before cleaning their stalls. The horses ate, and he taught me how to groom them and check their hooves for rocks. I watched Lucas brush the horses' manes with a thick comb.

"Now you try." He handed me the comb, and I ran it through the dark hair of a midnight black horse. The horse nuzzled against me. "You're a natural with horses," Lucas encouraged. I ducked my head as heat rose to my face.

"That's a beautiful ring." Lucas nodded toward my hand.

"Oh," I said, fidgeting with my ring. "A friend gave it to me." I hoped that was enough explanation and he wouldn't ask questions.

Lucas looked at the sky. "I wish you could stay here in the stables a little longer."

"Me, too," I said. "I need to go to the fields now, but I will be back tomorrow morning."

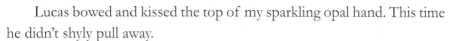
Lucas bowed and kissed the top of my sparkling opal hand. This time he didn't shyly pull away.

My face flamed with heat and I turned. "I'll see you tomorrow." I waved goodbye and raced toward the fields. I didn't want to be late on my first day.

A dozen people were already working in the field, including Master Fredrick. He was dressed like a commoner, in brown wool pants and a simple linen shirt. He and the other men rhythmically swung sickles back and forth, while the women gathered the wheat and tied it into bundles.

Fredrick walked toward me with a bright smile. Sweat stained the front of his shirt and glistened from his brow. "Hello, Auriella. Have you ever done this before?"

I shook my head. It didn't look any harder than swinging an axe to chop wood. I reached for the sickle in his hand. Fredrick recoiled it. "No, I would dream of making a lady. . ." He trailed off then pointed to the women. "You will gather the wheat. If you see farm animals or birds in the crops, just chase them out. Any questions?"

I could tell he was sincere, so I felt brave enough to ask, "Why are you dressed like a commoner? And Lucas," I pointed back at the stalls. "He was dressed like a peasant too."

"Working the land was father's idea. We've kept the tradition since he died. It's something we do to honor our father."

Fredrick tossed me a bundle of string to tie the wheat with, then walked away, whistling a cheery tune.

Tying wheat wasn't hard, but it was tedious, and every plant seemed to scratch into my skin. I did my best, but tied fewer bundles than the rest of the women. I tried not to be discouraged, but I really wanted to impress everyone on my first day.

Evening came and I went into the manor. I ate dinner in the kitchen with the cooks then helped scrub the dishes and floors before retiring to my room for the night.

I didn't know when I would be able to go to the Neviahan Circle and meet with Woldor the Wise. But it didn't matter anymore. I was human and I had a new normal life, just as I always wanted.

The warm months passed, and the harsh winter made farming impossible, which allowed me to spend more time with Lucas and the animals.

Lucas and I trudged along the frozen ground toward the stables. Our breath puffed above us like clouds, but somehow it seemed warmer when he was around. Long, amber grass protruded from the hard earth and crunched under our boots. I wrapped my wool scarf tighter around my face.

Lucas's smiling eyes peered at me between his scarf and hat. "So, you think you can best me this time?"

"I'm a better rider now. I practice when you're not watching," I said playfully.

Lucas laughed. His warm breath danced like fog above his head. He opened the stable doors and threw a saddle onto my favorite horse before tossing one onto his own. I buckled the straps. Lucas helped me onto my saddle before mounting his horse. I leaned forward and patted my mare's shimmering black coat.

Lucas grinned. "I will never forget how you screamed the first time you sat on a horse."

I thought back to the beginning of autumn. I had begged Lucas for weeks to teach me how to ride. When the chance finally came, I almost changed my mind.

Now, riding was second nature to me. We trotted to the edge of the

cow pasture at a calm pace. I gripped the reins with gloved hands.

"On your mark," Lucas started. "Get set. Go!" Lucas and I raced into the cow pasture to gather the cows before the storm set in. The last time we had played this game, I managed to get only one cow while Lucas gathered the rest of the herd.

I collected three cows and herded them toward the barn. I glanced over to see Lucas with seven. I veered toward another group of cows. The more cows I tried to gather, the harder it was to keep the herd under control. Lucas picked up a few of my strays and drove them into the barn. Again, I managed to bring in only one cow.

Lucas and I dismounted from our horses. He pushed his scarf under his chin and flashed a smile, as if hoping for my approval.

I unraveled my scarf from my face. "How do you get so many?" I was out of breath from the rush, but Lucas seemed invigorated by his victory.

"You have to use your voice and yell out, 'Yahh! Yahh!'"

I threw him a teasing smirk. "Now that I know your secret, I will beat you."

"Ah." Lucas smiled mischievously. "You are already faster when it comes to milking the cows. I can't have you best me with your herding skills as well."

He tossed me a wooden practice sword. I fumbled it before gaining control. "Let's see how much you've learned since our last lesson." Lucas flung his cloak aside, gripped his practice sword, and faced me in a stance.

I positioned my practice sword between us and returned his intense gaze. Our eyes locked and he growled. I laughed. If he was trying to intimidate me, that meant he was worried I could beat him.

He jabbed at me, and I hit his sword. He retaliated and swung at

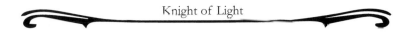

my legs. I stepped to the side and knocked the sword from his extended reach. It was a lucky shot, but I smiled, pretending I did it on purpose.

Lucas gave me a mock scowl. "I have been disarmed. It seems my pupil has learned as much as I." He raised his practice sword and attacked me afresh. We fought until the air grew colder and the dim winter light no longer shown between the cracks in the stable doors.

"It's getting late," I reluctantly said. We could practice all day during the winter, but the cooks expected me in the kitchen to clean up after dinner. Lucas's shoulders slumped.

"Don't worry. We can practice sword fighting tomorrow," I said.

Lucas sighed. "Tomorrow is Saturday."

"Oh, that's right." I bit my lip. I would be with Lady Hannah tomorrow and wouldn't see Lucas until Monday.

Like a gentleman, he placed my cloak over my shoulders. I wrapped the scarf around my face and pulled the hood over my head. Lucas pushed open the door.

"It's snowing," I said, taking in the magic of the moment.

Big flakes of snow floated from the sky and stuck to his beautiful eyelashes. "Wouldn't it be great if we got snowed in?" he asked. "Then we would get to spend the whole weekend together."

I laughed. "Like it's going to snow that much."

Lucas walked with me to the manor and escorted me to the kitchen. I took off my winter coat, scarf, and gloves, and tied an apron around my waist. Lucas lingered in the doorway, watching me as I piled the dishes next to the wash bucket.

"Oh, not you again, Master Lucas." The head cook scurried to the door and shooed him away. "How's the lady supposed to get any work done with you distracting her. It's a wonder you haven't gained weight

with how often you come looking for food when Auriella's on duty."

Lucas peered around the large woman and waved goodbye to me before she forced him out of the kitchen.

Winter passed too quickly and spring came along with the duties of sowing a crop. The orchards blossomed with pink and white fragrant flowers as the sun thawed the rich soil.

Lucas pulled me into the tree branches with him. It was our favorite place to have lunch before I headed to the farm to plant seeds. Lucas opened a sack of food and handed me a sandwich. "I'm glad you're not like other girls," Lucas said. "You're actually fun to be with."

I ate slowly. Next week I would turn fifteen. In a year, I would be eligible for courting. Did Lucas know this? Would he, the son of a lady, be interested in courting me, a handmaid? Would he wait for me to come of age? In town, I had seen the noble ladies dressed in fine, layered gowns with jewels in their hair. How could I compete with that? I wasn't literate or properly trained in etiquette. It was selfish for me to hope Lucas would choose me over the wealthy, educated, and beautiful noble maidens. The son of noble parents should court someone better than me.

At least, I thought both his parents were nobility. I knew who is mother was, but did know anything about his father.

"Lucas?" I hesitated, not meeting his eyes. "Who was your father?"

"My father. . ." Lucas looked away from me, and I immediately felt guilty for asking. "He was once a commoner, but he became a great knight for the king. The king gave him this land." He motioned toward the fields and orchards. "Then he was killed on a crusade. Mother cried for days when we got the letter from the king's messengers." Lucas picked at the bark on the tree then glanced at me with a spark in his eyes. "Someday, I want to become a great knight like my father, but a lot of things are

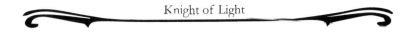

required before a person becomes a knight."

"Is sword fighting one of those things?" I leaned against a branch.

"Yes, it is." He looked at our practice swords on the ground. I could tell by the mischievous grin spreading across his face what he was thinking.

Lucas jumped.

I swung from the branches, dropped to the ground, and took up one of the swords. Lucas lunged with his sword extended. I parried his attack and thrust my sword toward his chest. Lucas blocked. He whirled his wooden sword toward my knees. I leapt over the blade, recovered, then sliced my sword through the air. Lucas went on the defense and blocked my attacks. I swung with all my strength. When I over-extended, Lucas stepped forward and tagged my arm with the tip of his sword.

"Gotcha," he called in triumph. Wiping the perspiration from his brow, he added, "You are getting very good."

"And you are getting very strong." I rubbed a tender spot on my left arm.

"I didn't hurt you, did I?" Lucas lowered his sword, stepped toward me and caressed my arm.

Nervous energy rushed through me, and my palms smoldered with heat. I pulled away from his touch. How could this be happening now? If flames came from my hands, Lucas would know I was different. I didn't want to ruin my new life at the manor. I had to get away. I turned from Lucas and sprinted toward the manor without looking back at him.

"I'm sorry," Lucas called.

Chapter Sixteen

A Life to Save

My heart pounded as I pushed open the door and entered Lady Hannah's room. "You wished to see me?" I shuffled my feet toward Lady Hannah's bed.

"Yes. I am going to reassign you to work in the kitchen permanently."

"What? Why?" I stammered. With shock running from the top of my head to my toes, I felt like I'd touched one of those horrible eels. To be assigned to the kitchen—away from Lucas—was the worst thing that could happen. Was it something I did?

"It's all right, my dear. Don't worry. You have done nothing wrong," Hannah said. "In fact, Lucas was quite put out when I told him I was reassigning you. He argued to have you stay and couldn't say enough about your work ethic and efficiency."

I bowed my head slightly to the regal lady. Some of the initial shock dissipated at the thought of Lucas fighting to have me near him. A coldness washed over me as Lady Hannah continued, "Nevertheless, you are

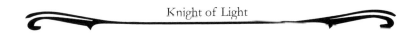

turning into a woman. Your place is in the manor, not herding cows and cleaning horse stalls. The kitchen staff loves you, and you will be happy there."

I tried to bite my tongue to keep the words from spilling out, but I couldn't help myself. "Lucas has taught me well, but I still have so much to learn—"

Lady Hannah cut me off. "I know you and Lucas are friends, but he needs to be more respectful and understand your place in society as a woman."

I lowered my head. Tears burned at my eyes. I clenched my shirt, my fingers smoldered. I quickly released my skirt and clasped my hands together before I caught my dress on fire. I bit on my tongue and tried to numb my aching heart and suppress the fire inside me. Catching on fire now wouldn't help me earn a place in society–even if my place was to be just a servant. What Lady Hannah probably meant, was that I needed to be more respectful of Lucas's place as a noble in society. The noble maidens were coming around more and Lucas hadn't made himself available to court them like his brothers had.

Hannah continued, "You two will still see each other and maintain your friendship. My son has been happy and hasn't complained once about his duties since you've been helping him. Yet, it is time for you to focus on more appropriate responsibilities."

I did not speak, for fear I might seem ungrateful for all Lady Hannah had done for me. I nodded, turned to the door, and returned to my room.

From my bedroom window, I watched Lucas trudge from the stables toward the manor. He looked devastated, and his steps didn't have the same energetic bounce I was used to seeing. I flew down the flight of stairs and greeted him at the door.

His eyes lit up, and he raced to meet me. "Did Mother talk to you?" Lucas asked.

I nodded and dropped my head so he wouldn't see the tears that were starting to form.

He continued, "I tried to change her mind. She doesn't understand—"

I raised my hand to stop him. "I have an idea." I winked.

Lucas smirked. "I know you're planning something sneaky when you smile like that."

Over the next few months, I found ways to spend time with Lucas. I arose early in the mornings to go riding or to practice sword fighting with Lucas. In the afternoons, I got permission from the head cook to eat my lunch outside.

One particular morning, Lucas joined me in the orchard treetops and, as usual, walked me back to the kitchen after we ate. When Lucas and I entered the kitchen all the cooks went silent. They had probably been gossiping about one of Lucas's brothers and didn't want him to overhear.

"Will I see you tomorrow?" Lucas asked.

"Of course," I answered.

Lucas's lips tightened like he was holding back a grin, then quickly turned and left.

I knelt down and scooped ash from the oven while the cooks continued their gossiping about people in the manor. I tuned them out and daydreamed that by some miracle Lucas and I could get married next year when I turned sixteen.

"It is too bad about Lady Hannah," the head cook said.

The statement shook me from my fantasy. "What's wrong with Lady Hannah?"

"She keeps getting worse and worse since her dear husband's death,"

she answered. "Her health has been going downhill. If she keeps on like she is, she won't be around for much longer."

My heart sank. I scooped out another pile of ash from the cool oven and dumped it into the waste bucket. I wished I had Hazella's book of cures. There had to be some herb or berry that could heal Lady Hannah.

I remembered flipping through the pages, admiring the art and the picture of the ruby necklace on the last page.

"The necklace!" I shouted.

The head cook put her hands on her hips. "What are you going on about, child?"

"I . . . uh," I stammered and picked at my fingers. "I need to be excused. It's an emergency. I promise I'll return in time to take Lady Hannah her dinner." I didn't wait for the cook to answer before I burst from the door and hurried to Ruburt's blacksmith shop. Cassi floated overhead, watching Ruburt straighten out a shield.

"Ruburt, do you remember where the ruby necklace is?" I asked.

Ruburt thought before his eyes flashed with remembrance. "It's with the bags of coins."

"Will you get it for me?" I pleaded. "Will you get it for me quickly?"

Ruburt groaned. "Fredrick needs me to work on some armor for his jousting tournament. I fixed the plows and, apparently, he was impressed. Now he wants me to pound out the dents in his shield after each jousting practice. I guess I'm the armor and weapon smith now too."

I paced the room. "Lady Hannah is ill, and the necklace is the only thing I can think of that might help."

Ruburt crossed his arms in front of his chest. "It may not work. Hazella had a lot of tricks she conjured up just for the money. She cheated people into thinking she had a cure for whatever illness they had."

"But Hazella wanted it for herself. It must do something good to the wearer." I turned to Cassi. "May I use the necklace and see if it will help?"

Cassi shrugged her shoulders. "Cassi needs no more. Necklace can be Auriella's now."

"Thank you, Cassi. That's very kind of you."

"Fine," Ruburt said. "It'll take me 'bout an hour to go and retrieve it from its hiding place. I've moved the coins and Cassi's necklace to a new hiding place with all my other treasure."

"All your other treasure?" I gasped. With just the gold coins he took from Hazella he had enough money to start a new life if he wanted to. What else was in his hiding place?

"I like to collect treasure," Ruburt said in a tone that sounded like I should have already known. "That's what dwarves do. Once I think of something worth making, I'll melt the gold and make it. Until then, I'm perfectly happy staying in the safety of the manor. But if you need Cassi's necklace, I'll make a special trip to get it for you." He leaned forward and whispered. "Have you gone to the stone circle yet and met with Woldor?"

I shook my head. I hated being reminded that I still needed to meet with the Neviahan historian. "I will, after I give Lady Hannah the necklace," I promised.

"Then I'll meet you at the manor in a few hours with the necklace."

I took a deep breath. "Thank you, Ruburt."

I returned to the kitchen and finished my chores while the cooks prepared dinner. After several hours of worrying, I heard Ruburt's footsteps echo on the stairs. I bounded from the room and met him at the door. "Did you get the treasure?" I asked.

Ruburt put his finger over his lips. "Shhh!" His eyes darted around wildly at all the cooks.

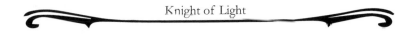

I covered my mouth and followed him up the stairs to the drawing room. Ruburt shut the door and pushed it to make sure it was tightly closed. He reached into a pouch, pulled out the necklace, and handed it to me. I touched the brilliant ruby embedded in the gold and silver pendent.

"I also brought with me the last link." Ruburt pulled out a tiny pair of tongs. I handed Ruburt the necklace, and he connected the last link. "There, it's finished." Ruburt scowled. "It doesn't look magical, but at least the craftsmanship is good."

"You did a wonderful job, Ruburt. Now, to find out if it works." I slid the necklace into my pocket and returned to the kitchen. I could feel every eye in the room on me as I picked up the silver tray with Lady Hannah's dinner. "I will return after delivering this meal," I said casually. I was pleased with how calm my voice sounded despite the anxiety I felt.

The necklace weighed down my apron pocket as I balanced the silver tray in my hands. Two handmaids walked beside me to attend to Lady Hannah. I had to be alone when I gave Lady Hannah the necklace. Someone might get the wrong idea if they saw a servant with such a valuable item. "I hope this works," I mumbled to myself.

A handmaid opened the door. I carried the tray across the room and set it on Lady Hannah's lap. I turned and headed for the door, trying to appear as if I was returning to the kitchen as usual, but I stopped at the window and slipped behind one of the navy curtains. It seemed like forever before the handmaids left the room and Lady Hannah fell asleep.

I crept out from behind the curtain and tiptoed across the room until I stood over Lady Hannah's bed. I pulled the necklace from my pocket, one link at a time. What was I doing? I caught myself. I clutched the necklace to my chest. If I wanted people to think I was normal, I shouldn't be sneaking around with magical objects. I should just follow orders and

return to my duties in the kitchen.

I turned to retreat, but stopped. What if this necklace could heal her? Would trying to help her be worth the risk of losing my job, my home, and my new family? What if the necklace worked and they thought I was a witch? I was on treacherous ground as it was. With all the emotions that had seized me lately, it was becoming more and more difficult to hide my fiery power and pretend to be normal.

I turned back to Lady Hannah. I couldn't let her die if I held the cure in my hand. I lowered the necklace to Hannah's chest and slipped it around her frail neck. If I was going to be safe from judgment while helping her, she couldn't know it was me who gave it to her. I held my breath. My fingers felt stubby as I tried to connect the clasp. I pulled away, but my finger tugged on the chain.

Lady Hannah awoke. Her tired eyes filled with question. "What are you doing in here, Auriella?"

My heart raced. "I . . . I heard you were sick. I want to help you get better."

Lady Hannah looked at the necklace. "Where did you get such an item? You didn't steal it, did you?"

"No! No! I'm not a thief. It's my necklace. A friend gave it to me. I think it's a healing necklace." This was horrible. The story didn't sound convincing, even to me.

Hannah examined the necklace and the concern melted from her face. "Auriella, this is a beautiful necklace, but it will not make me well. I appreciate your kind gesture, but I am too far gone." She closed her eyes. "Nothing can heal me now."

How could Lady Hannah be giving up so easily after all the trouble and risk I took to help? "You have done so much for me. Please let me

give you this necklace and see if it makes you feel better," I pleaded.

Lady Hannah's ashen face beamed with compassion. She patted my curls, which now reached my shoulders, and agreed, "If it would make you happy, I will wear your beautiful necklace."

I sighed with relief and wiped my eyes on my sleeve. Even if the necklace didn't heal Lady Hannah, at least I had made her smile. "If I had a mother, I would want her to be like you," I gushed, overwhelmed with a feeling I'd never experienced before.

Color washed over Lady Hannah's face, brightening her cheeks. Lady Hannah pushed herself up in a seated position. "Do you know why I took you in?" she asked.

I shook my head.

"Before my sons were born I had a baby girl. She was born early and only lived a few hours. She had red hair like yours. If she had lived, I hope she would have been like you."

Chapter Seventeen
Lady Auriella

I still worried for Lady Hannah. I lay awake for several hours, then, my sleep was restless when I did fall asleep. I had trouble pulling myself out of bed in the morning and didn't have time for my secret sword fighting practice with Lucas. I was already late for breakfast preparations.

I pulled a skirt over my long under-dress and tied an apron around my waist. I sped through the hallway and down the stairs to the kitchen. Breakfast was almost ready. I dropped my shoulders.

"Sorry I'm late."

"Sword fighting with Lucas again?" one of the cooks asked.

"What? How did you know about that?" It was supposed to be a secret. Lucas and I had been so sneaky.

They giggled in chorus.

"No, I wasn't with Lucas. I overslept."

"You needed it," The head cook said. "You're staying up too late and getting up too early to sword fight."

It was impossible to keep anything from them. The king should hire the lot of them as spies for the military. I pulled myself together and headed for the pile of pots next to the wash bucket. I scrubbed the dishes while the cooks gossiped about various people and things.

"Lady Hannah!" one of the cooks exclaimed. I spun around. Lady Hannah stood in the doorway. Her auburn hair glistened, and her skin radiated a warm glow. I hardly recognized her.

The cooks froze in place and stared at the queenly, youthful woman. Judging from the cooks' reaction, none of them had ever seen her like this, at least not for a very long time.

I wiped my soapy wet hands on my apron. It hit me at once. The necklace was more powerful than I thought. I had used it without any idea as to what kind of power it held. It could have done something horrible to Lady Hannah. It could have killed her or changed her into a monster. I clenched my jaw. Even though this looked like a good thing on the surface, Lady Hannah's change was too drastic. People were sure to be suspicious. This was, by far, the worst thing I'd ever done.

"Auriella, come with me. I need to speak with you," Lady Hannah commanded.

I lowered my head and followed Lady Hannah to the east wing of the manor. What if they accused me of witchcraft and tried to burn me to death? Once my skin wouldn't burn, they would know my secret. I was doomed. There were too many witnesses. I couldn't hide and this problem wasn't going to disappear. I fidgeted with the rainbow ring on my hand. I won't run, I decided. I deserved whatever punishment Hannah sentenced me to.

We entered the vast private family library. The room was as tall as three houses, and as long as a small pasture. Bookshelves lined the walls.

Four massive, stained glass windows hung like lighted artwork, shooting rainbow light throughout the room. I forgot my fears and took in the splendor of the library.

Lady Hannah glided to a big table piled with papers and sat in a large, plush chair. Her cheeks were full of color. Her blue eyes were clear and bright.

My fingers trembled as I smoothed out my dress. Lady Hannah obviously had something important to say, but she just stared at me. I mustered the courage to break the silence with the truth. "The necklace is magical. I only wanted to help. I didn't mean for it to—"

"The ruby necklace has healed me." Lady Hannah wiped her eyes and touched the necklace. "The necklace is truly a gift. I feel like dancing and running." Lady Hannah grasped my hands. "You have been such a blessing to this family, and the manor staff adores you. I have thought about your situation and what I could do to reward you for all the good you have done."

Lady Hannah paused and sighed. "I remembered you have no family and only a little education. I have given you a job and a place to stay, but you have given me a new life. Now I want to offer you a new life as well."

I tried to digest the information. So far, all I understood was that she wasn't mad and I wasn't going to be executed.

"I want to adopt you," Lady Hannah said. "You will be a legal heir with my sons and have a noble title."

I gasped. "You mean, you will be my mother now?"

Lady Hannah nodded. "I will be the closest thing to a mother the law will allow." I sat in silence, stunned by what Lady Hannah offered. Lady Hannah continued, "Now, Lady Auriella, you must remember that with a title comes leadership and responsibility. I cannot have you running

around the estate uneducated. You will have tutors to teach you grammar, the arts, and etiquette."

My heart pounded inside my chest and pulsed in my ears. My throat caught so I couldn't speak. Lady Hannah was offering me a part of her estate, and, yet it was all a mistake. I wasn't worthy. I hadn't done anything to deserve this. It was a mistake.

"I have spent the morning preparing the papers to make it proper and legal for you to be a joint heir with my sons. Once they are signed, I will send them to London where the king will mark them with his seal."

I put one hand on my forehead. I wiped my clammy hands on my skirt. King Henry, himself, would approve this? I blinked hard several times to be sure I was actually awake.

"As you get older, you will fully understand the meaning of this gift. Will this be all right with you?" Lady Hannah smiled and patted my hand.

"Oh, yes, yes, yes!" I answered. I would become a lady and have a noble title. Most of all, I would have someone who would be like a real mother to me.

Lady Hannah clapped her hands three times, and her sons entered the room. Apparently, the servants had called for them earlier and had given them instructions to come in their best clothing. I blushed deeply when Lucas entered wearing the dashing formal tunic he wore only for special occasions. Each of the boys' faces filled with surprise when they saw their mother. They hadn't seen her out of her bed for months, and probably not as youthful since they were toddlers.

"Mother?" Alwaien asked. "What . . ." His mouth hung open, frozen in speech.

Lady Hannah held up her hand. Delight rang clear in her youthful voice. "I'm sure you want to know why I have called this family meeting.

It is the blessing of Heaven that my health has improved drastically during the night. I would like you to meet the angel who has helped me—a new member of our family, Lady Auriella."

I slumped like a guilty bandit who had just been caught. I hoped my name wouldn't be associated at all with her healing. I certainly didn't want anyone thinking I'd done something magical.

Lady Hannah didn't seem to notice my panic. She continued her explanation to her sons. "Documents have been prepared to ensure she will receive her noble title. I will need each of you to sign the papers as witnesses."

"Noble title?" Alwaien protested. "But she is a servant! There is not one drop of noble blood in her. She's an orphan."

"I'm her new mother," Hannah said. Her eyes were bright, but they took on a stare as fierce as that of a lioness.

"But, you're not her real mother?" Lucas asked in a small voice. "I mean, she won't be my sister. Will she?" He looked terrified, and I wanted to cry. Why was he taking the same side as Alwaien? Why was he resisting having me as a part of his family?

"She will be a joint heir," Hannah explained.

Lucas exhaled deeply and smiled at me. "That will be wonderful."

Alwaien glared at me as if I had stolen something from him. Fredrick was relaxed and nonchalant about the whole issue and Lucas seemed to be going along with this willingly, now that he knew I wouldn't be his "real sister."

Lady Hannah lifted a long, feathered pen and reached for her magnifying glass. She looked through the glass, laughed, and tossed it aside. "I don't need this anymore." Lady Hannah signed, then handed the pen to me. "You need to sign as well."

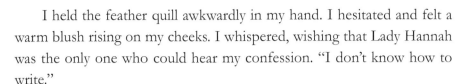

I held the feather quill awkwardly in my hand. I hesitated and felt a warm blush rising on my cheeks. I whispered, wishing that Lady Hannah was the only one who could hear my confession. "I don't know how to write."

Lady Hannah nodded. "Just do your best."

I marked the parchment with several loops for my signature.

I was still in too much shock to feel any emotion, but, as soon as I saw tears glistening in Hannah's eyes, I broke down in tears too. She held me in a strong, comforting hug. "Welcome to our family, Lady Auriella."

Things were different after that day. Despite my new duties and hours of schooling, I continued to rise early and secretly practice sword fighting with Lucas. Both of us were strong and clever with the sword. Lucas assured me our relationship wouldn't change just because I was a Lady and joint heir now. Secretly, I hoped my new title and status put me on even grounds with the other eligible noble maidens.

I loved my new classes. I spent hours studying how to behave like a lady as well as both modern and ancient art and the history of the world. What excited me most was that I finally learned to read and write. I stayed up at night, pouring over books in the family library until the candles were nothing but pools of wax. I read about religion, geography, history, and government.

My cozy new room was next to the library. A beautiful mahogany-framed mirror hung on the wall and a warm fire blazed in the fireplace next to the balcony. A wardrobe burst with fine gowns and slippers.

Like most autumn evenings, Cassi and Ruburt joined me in my room after supper. Cassi sat on the dresser and played with my jewelry. I lay on the scarlet rug carpeting my floor, while Ruburt tinkered with a metal trap.

"I haven't been able to get all my work done during daylight hours."

Ruburt looked at Cassi and scowled. "That pixie is always pulling me away from my duties and having me chase after squirrels and phantoms."

Cassi placed a ring on her head like a crown and blew a raspberry at him. Ruburt pointed to one of his tools. I stood and retrieved it for him. He adjusted the trap door and groaned. "Cassi thinks she's seeing Shadow Wolves in the woods again."

"What?" I almost shouted. "They wouldn't come this close to the manor, would they?"

"If there's something they want, they will," Ruburt said.

I tightened my jaw. "I haven't created fire in over a year. I'm human now, Ruburt."My voice quivered. I hoped Ruburt didn't sense my own misgivings. I wanted my words to be true. I wanted to be human, and I wasn't about to tell Ruburt about the many close calls of fire bursting from my hands, especially when Lucas was around.

Ruburt shook his head. "You don't suddenly turn into a human."

"How do you know?" I tried not to sound defensive, but I had a wonderful life, and I would do anything to protect it. I twisted the rainbow ring on my finger.

"There's only one way to know for sure. You need to go to the Neviahan stone circle and summon Woldor in the morning. It's time."

He was right. It was time. The days and months had passed. I had tried to put that task out of my mind. With the Shadow Legion still looking for me, I couldn't hold back any longer.

I hesitated. What if Woldor said I was a Neviahan? Would I have to leave my home and all my new friends? I thought quickly. "I can't go. I have sword practice with Lucas in the morning. He will worry for me."

Ruburt looked away and mumbled, "That boy is always looking for excuses to be with you. I think he's in love with you."

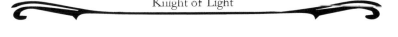

"Oh no, not Lucas. We are just friends. If he was in love with me, I'd know." I unsuccessfully tried to hold back a smile from spreading across my face. I secretly wished Lucas was in love with me.

Ruburt laughed and continued to work on the trap door of the cage. "Suit yourself."

A faint knock came on the door. I jumped. Every time the subject of the Shadow Legion came up it put me on edge for days. I rose to answer the door. A warm light from a lamp lit Lucas's smiling face. My heart raced. What did he have to say that couldn't wait until practice tomorrow morning?

"Hello." Lucas shuffled his feet and looked at the ground.

"Good evening," I replied with a curtsy. Why did he come here and why was he whispering? Something must be terribly wrong. "Are you all right? Please, come in." I tried to sound calm.

"No, thank you." He lifted his eyes and smiled, melting away my fear. "There is something I need to tell you."

"What is it?" I asked. Lucas was always full of surprises and new adventures. Maybe he discovered a new way to disarm people. What if one of the cows gave birth to a new calf? What if—?

Lucas reached out, grabbed my waist, and pulled me to him. His lips pressed against mine.

My eyes stayed wide open in amazement. My knees weakened, my hands shook, but the rest of my body froze. I stood like a statue, not knowing what to say or think, not daring to pull away. In those a few seconds, my wonderful relationship with Lucas evolved into something deeper and more complex.

Lucas stepped back, grinning from ear to ear. Without saying another word, he turned and fled down the hallway like a thief. His footfalls

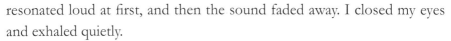

resonated loud at first, and then the sound faded away. I closed my eyes and exhaled quietly.

Cassi buzzed around the room and laughed. She flew to me and giggled. "Kissy! Kissy!" I ignored her and stared down the hall. My cheeks ached from the intense smile that spread across my face.

Ruburt shook me. "Auriella, are you all right?"

I blushed. "What just happened?" Did Lucas really just steal a kiss? "I think he might be in love with me." I fell onto the bed.

"Humph!" Ruburt declared. "Of course he is. And, the way those cooks gossip, the whole manor knows he's in love with you."

"What? Everyone knows?" I gripped the end of my bed. "How could've everyone known but me?" I leapt off the bed and stood as regally as I could. "That's fine. I don't care if they know." I tried to sound like I didn't care, but my new romantic secret had already been exposed. My tough façade melted away. I giggled and danced around the room with my arms outstretched. "You know what? I think I might be in love with him too."

Cassi cheered and danced in the air above me. Pixie dust showered down on me as I pirouetted in the sparkling gold flakes.

Ruburt sighed, shrugged his stocky shoulders, and shook his head. "Young'uns and pixies."

Chapter Eighteen
Wolder the Wise

I awoke the next morning and put my fingers to my lips. I couldn't believe Lucas had kissed me. I savored the memory before I finally arose, floated to the balcony doors, and pushed them opened. The dawn soaked me in warmth. My skin shimmered and scattered the light like the sun hitting a thousand mirrors.

The golden and scarlet leaves of the trees fell to the earth and carpeted my balcony. There was something magical about the seasons changing, and I couldn't help but feel a wonderful change was about to happen in my own life.

With the coming of autumn, also came the harvest festival. People from all over the country traveled to Oswestry to trade and sell their produce, crafts, and livestock. Traveling troubadours and mercenaries visited the festival with songs and stories of knights and distant kingdoms.

This year, Lady Hannah dedicated the celebration in honor of the bounteous blessings which had come to the manor. To the amazement of

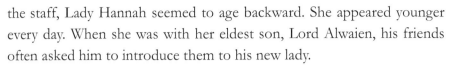

the staff, Lady Hannah seemed to age backward. She appeared younger every day. When she was with her eldest son, Lord Alwaien, his friends often asked him to introduce them to his new lady.

From my window, I watched the riders and horses warming up in the jousting arena. This year's jousting events were special. Lady Hannah's son, Frederick, would be knighted and would participate in his first joust.

A knock fell on my door, interrupting my thoughts. "Lucas," I whispered. A thrill raced through me. I tossed on a dress, darted to the mirror, brushed back my hair, then dashed to the door. I composed myself, then pulled it open.

My shoulders dropped. "Oh, it's only you, Ruburt."

Ruburt looked at me with a scowl. "Who were you expecting? Your knight in shining armor?"

"Well, yes. Lucas and I are going to practice this morning."

Ruburt shook his head. "You're the most distracted girl I've ever met. You can't keep avoiding Woldor forever. Remember what the fairy queen told you? Remember that 'em Shadow Wolves are still hunting you. I know you want to be normal, Auriella, but the truth is, you're not."

I took a deep breath. It was true. Whatever Woldor said couldn't be good news. My head spun. It was only a matter of time before the Shadow Wolves returned. This time, Shadow Lords and maybe the Shadow King, Erebus, could be with them. Hazella was probably searching for me too.

"Ruburt," my voice broke with emotion, "I'm afraid."

Ruburt's face softened.

"I'm afraid of who I am." The tears flowed freely down my cheeks. I wrapped my arms around my waist. What if I was the Lady of Neviah? What would that mean? Would I still get to stay at the manor with Lady Hannah and Lucas, or would I have to return to The Great Kingdom of

Neviah? Would my new family still love me if I wasn't human?

I once would have given anything to leave Earth and go to a magic kingdom, but now that things were easy in my life, I wanted to stay. I had a noble title, lived in a manor, wore nice clothes, and had respect from the community. Everything was perfect.

If the Shadow Legion came looking for me in Oswestry, would the manor guard be able to defend us? I doubted all the armies of England could stand against such a force. Ruburt once said I could destroy the Rebellion, that I must stop them.

I fell onto my bed and buried my face in the pillow.

I felt Ruburt's hand on my back. "There's only one way to know for sure. Woldor will tell you who you are. It's better to know than to wonder. Maybe he'll tell you what to do and how to protect the manor. What if you are stronger than the greatest knight in England?"

I turned my head and met Ruburt's eyes. "Ruburt, I'm afraid of how strong I am. Did you see what I did to that Shadow Wolf? Did you see the shadow fiend writhing in the flames? It was awful. What if I lost control and accidently did that to someone I love?"

Ruburt looked thoughtful. "The more you learn about your power the less afraid you'll be. You need to be prepared, so the next time there's an attack, you won't faint in the middle of battle."

I sat up, brushed my hair back, and looked at Ruburt. "Promise me that no matter what Woldor says, you will still be my friend."

"Of course," Ruburt said.

"And, please, please don't say anything to Lucas."

Ruburt patted my hand. "I wouldn't dream of saying anything to anyone. Let's get Cassi and leave quickly before anything else gets in the way."

I let out a long sigh after holding my breath. "We should leave before

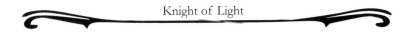

Lucas comes, and I have to explain to him where we are going."

I threw a traveling cloak over my shoulders and snuck through the manor to the stables. I mounted my glossy, midnight-black horse. Ruburt got on his pony and Cassi flew overhead as we rode toward the stone circle at the edge of the valley.

The valley where the wolves tracked us didn't look as intimidating on a clear day. The Neviahan circle of stones rose up on the tallest hill. The altar in the center of the circle glinted in the sunlight. My heart thumped in my chest. I had avoided this meeting for too long. It was time to learn the truth.

I dismounted outside the circle.

"I can't go in the circle with you," Ruburt said. "Only the Neviahans can enter."

I hoped Ruburt was being overly dramatic. I stepped into the circle and expected something spectacular to happen, but nothing did. I walked to the moss-covered altar and brushed my hand across the smooth surface.

I turned to Ruburt and asked, "What am I supposed to do?"

Ruburt shrugged.

We waited in silence. Every minute that passed became more awkward.

"Woldor the Wise isn't here." I headed for my horse. What if I had waited too long?

The wind blew and the trees swayed back and forth. White clouds billowed in the eastern sky. I froze in place. This couldn't be good.

"Lookie see!" Cassi pointed to the sky.

Out of the storm soared a huge, emerald creature. Its bat-like wings extended from its body. A long tail flowed behind it like a ribbon. The massive creature dove toward us in gentle swoops and prepared to land.

Hard plates armored his chest, and scales covered his body like lizard skin.

Ruburt shook his head and mumbled, "Impossible."

The ancient dragon landed in the circle next to the altar and towered over me. I should have been more terrified, but something inside caused me to stand my ground.

The dragon tilted his head to get a better look at me. Our eyes met, and my heart beat fiercely. The dragon bowed his head. "The Lady of Neviah has finally come."

Ruburt's eyes glistened with tears, and he reverently bowed. Cassi still grinned like nothing had changed.

I froze in awe. Everything I had tried to cover, all my concerns about being different, all my hopes for being human—the life and identity I had assumed—all of it was dashed and rearranged. The dragon exposed the truth I tried to hide from.

Now that I knew the dragon could speak, I asked, "Are you here to take me to Woldor the Wise?"

"My dear, lady," the dragon said, seeming to smile. "I am Woldor the Wise."

I tightened my jaw to keep it from dropping.

"Don't be afraid," Woldor said. "Even if I wanted to, I have not the power to destroy you. Your Neviahan gifts are far more than merely wielding the fire element."

I opened my mouth to speak, but didn't know what question to ask first.

The dragon continued. "As the Lady of Neviah, you have been given the same power that runs through the veins of the great kings and queens of your home world."

Even though my heart, and everything within in me, told me it was

true, I still couldn't see myself as someone so powerful. "How can I be the Lady of Neviah?" I strained to keep my voice from quivering.

Woldor chuckled and smoke trickled from his nose. "Now, come, Auriella. Climb on my back. I have a few things to teach you about your powers and your Neviahan heritage."

I stepped forward and looked at Ruburt for approval. Ruburt seemed surprised that I would even question, and he motioned for me to go.

I reached out and touched Woldor's warm, scaly skin. Gathering my courage, I grasped the dragon's shoulder blade and pulled myself onto his back. So much for being a normal girl – normal girls don't ride dragons.

I nestled into a spot above his wings, then leaned forward over the dragon's broad back and gripped tightly with my legs. I was careful not to lean back on the wings or forward onto the sharp horns lining the dragon's head.

Even with scales and sharp horns surrounding me, I somehow felt as comfortable riding the dragon as I was my own horse. Woldor flapped his massive wings and rose off the ground. The stone circle and Oswestry seemed to shrink below as the dragon gained altitude.

Chapter Nineteen

Dragon Cave

The air grew thin and cold. I gripped the dragon tighter and huddled close to his warm body. The world below looked small and far away, but somehow, I felt closer to home in the heavens. Woldor caught a current of wind and glided along smoothly. The rhythm of the colossal beast's wings caused him to soar with grace.

I drew in a deep breath and tossed my head back, letting the wind tousle my hair. Soft white clouds carpeted the sky beneath me, blocking my view of Earth. The garden of billowing cotton gave the illusion that I could step off the dragon's back and stand firmly on top of the cloudbank.

In the distance, a high mountain peak rose from the sea of clouds like a granite monument. Gray slabs of jagged stone fortified the mountain. Woldor veered toward a cave and landed with a great thud. Loose rocks sprinkled down the mountainside. I slid off the dragon's back and followed him into the belly of the mountain.

Woldor took a deep breath. As he exhaled a flame sprang from his mouth, lighting a torch on the wall. Candles stood scattered across an oak desk. Shelves lined the room and held books, scrolls, maps, and artifacts. "Come and sit," Woldor offered.

I climbed on the oversized chair at the table as Woldor searched through a stack of scrolls. While my breathing and heart rate were even and calm, the questions continued to rage through my head.

The first question I wanted to ask was, "Are you sure this isn't some kind of mistake?" Could I actually be the Lady of Neviah or even a Neviahan? It would take a lot more sword practicing before I could hold off even a small army, let alone the entire Shadow Legion.

I let the questions roll around in my head, but kept them to myself. I did finally ask, "What is all this stuff?" I pointed to a silver sphere lined with a band of sapphires. Runes marked the globe as if it were a language from another world.

"That, my dear, is a compass that works only by faith, a trinket that came with one of the Neviahan records."

I tilted my head. It didn't look anything like a compass to me.

"We dragons are the guardians of ancient records and treasure. I have been given the task of guarding the records of Neviah and the treasure of Ophir and Kolob."

I nodded and pretended I knew what he just said.

"Aha! Here it is!" he said in triumph. Woldor lifted a leather-bound book with gold leaf embossing accenting the cover. "This is the record of the Great Kingdom of Neviah, the Neviahans' journey to Earth, and the war with Erebus." Woldor blew the dust from the book, creating a small whirlwind. I sneezed several times.

Woldor chuckled a low throaty laugh. "You should see what happens

when I sneeze."

"I can only imagine." I grinned.

He opened the book and placed a large pair of spectacles on the end of his nose. "Now let me see . . . here we are." He turned from the book and looked at me above his reading glasses. "In order to help you understand your mission, I am going to tell you about the ancient world, before the great flood. Yes, I am that old. Thousands of years ago, the Earth was one continent, called Pangaea. It looked almost identical to Neviah."

"So, Earth is a lot like the Great Kingdom of Neviahan?" I asked, wanting to make sure I understood.

Woldor nodded. "It was, before the Shadow Legion invaded Earth, that is." He paused and his eyes glistened with sorrow. "In the Great Kingdom of Neviah, a powerful man, called Erebus, caused an uprising. Erebus used his skills to gather followers and caused a revolt against the kingdom.

"Those who resisted fought against the Rebellion and drove them out. Then the King of Neviah banished the Erebus and his followers. The rebels' inner light faded, leaving only shadows. That's why people call them the Shadow Legion."

My hands unconsciously clenched my dress as I listened.

"Defeated and enraged, Erebus and the Shadow Legion came to Earth to establish their own Dark Neviah. To create their kingdom, all the Shadows had to do was eliminate the planet's governing race–the humans."

I leaned forward and interjected. "But shadows can't hurt anyone." It wasn't so much of a statement as a plea.

Woldor shook his head. "I wish that were true. Since the Shadows no longer had physical bodies, they tried to steal the bodies of other

creatures, such as serpents and arachnids. Alas, eventually a human was persuaded by the faint whisperings of Erebus, himself. This man became envious of his brother's wife. Erebus whispered into his ear and told him if he killed his brother, then she would be his. When the man obeyed, his body was breached, and Erebus took control."

I put my fingertips to my teeth.

"Over a period of time, Erebus helped a small number of Shadow Spirits do the same. Once they inhabited a human body, the Shadow Spirit became a Shadow Lord. The Shadow Lords help their army multiply by stealing identities and recruiting humans to their cause by preying on their human weaknesses."

I gripped the table. "Why would a human join them?"

"Power," Woldor answered in a rumbling growl. "They joined because they believed Erebus would grant them power."

I shook my head. Hazella wanted power from the Rebellion. My muscles tensed, but I tried to sound brave. "So the Shadow Legionnaires all have bodies again?"

Woldor put a clawed finger up. "Not all of them. Most of them are still Shadows looking for weak humans to entice."

"So, how do we fight them?" I asked.

"The King of Neviah prepared the kingdom's strongest warriors for Earth combat. He sent them to this planet disguised as human beings and born to human parents."

I shook my head. "But if I'm Neviahan, how come I don't remember all of this?"

Woldor set the book back on the shelf. "Human memories are more intense than Neviahan memories. After a year or two as human beings, your memory of Neviah fades. It's an unfortunate disadvantage you have

in the battle against Erebus. The Shadow Legionnaires still have their memories of Neviah and the war." Woldor looked at me from above his glasses. "They even remember who you are."

I sat on my hands, as if trying to hide my power of fire. "It's not fair," I whispered.

Woldor's eyes sparkled from behind his glasses. "No, Erebus doesn't fight fair, and he shows no mercy. That's why it's important for you to rediscover who you are and learn to use your powers. You have no choice but to fight. Don't be afraid of your gifts. Not using them is one of the worst things you can do. The Shadow Legion is jealous of your gifts, and they will try to take your powers from you."

I pulled my knees to my chest. "How will they try to take my powers?"

"The Neviahans are stronger than the enemy, but if a member of the Shadow Legion is clever enough to kill a Neviahan they cannot steal their image the way they steal human identities. Instead, they drink the Neviahan's blood and steal some of their power."

My stomach tightened. "If Neviahans are so much stronger, then how can they kill us?" As soon as I'd asked, I wondered if I really wanted to know.

Woldor let out a deep sigh. "Not long ago, Erebus killed a Neviahan warrior. The Neviahan warrior had tremendous physical strength, but a beautiful woman enticed him. He let down his guard and ignored the warning signs. His loss was devastating. Not only did we lose a good warrior, but Erebus stole the Neviahan's great strength from his blood."

My mind raced over the information. There was no use in pretending I wasn't Neviahan anymore. Even if I decided not to fight this battle, the Shadow Legion would always be after me. I couldn't hide. I had no choice but to fight.

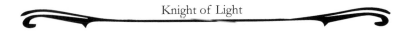

I could do this—I had to.

"Will I be alone?" I asked.

"No." His answer didn't hold any doubt. "There are others out there, like you, discovering their powers at a young age and preparing for war against the Shadow Legion."

I exhaled and dropped my shoulders. I wasn't an abomination of nature, demon spawn, or witch. I was just me, a Neviahan, and I wasn't alone.

"Come with me." Woldor nodded toward the entrance. "I will return you to the Neviahan Circle. Protect your identity. Your human body is the best disguise for your warrior spirit as you prepare for the time when you must face the Rebellion."

I followed Woldor out of the cave and stood with him on the high mountain ledge. A cool gust hit me, and I took in a breath of mountain air. I had a human body with human memories and the capacity to love the way humans did, but deep inside me, a Neviahan soul of fire smoldered.

I mounted Woldor's back, and we dove into the sky. The bright sun warmed my face, contrasting the cold air streaming past me. I carefully laid my head against the dragon's neck and imagined myself as a great warrior. I had more questions now than before I left. With my mind sorting out all the new information, the time passed and soon we landed in the Neviahan Circle outside Oswestry.

Ruburt and Cassi still waited for me just outside the circle.

I slid off the dragon's back and Woldor gave me one last caution. "Stay on your guard. The Shadow Legion is gathering strength and getting ready to strike. Earth is not your home – it's your battlefield."

I smiled bravely, though my heart swelled with new doubts.

"Your heart is like that old compass you saw," he said. "Have faith, and you will be guided to where you need to go."

Chapter Twenty

Tournament

I had a lot to think about when I returned home, and some explaining to do about why I had been absent a whole day before the jousting tournament. Everyone seemed satisfied with the explanation of needing some time to myself to figure out who I really am. Apparently, many girls my age go through the same thing.

On the day of the jousting event, the town was in a frenzy. I searched the manor for Lucas and passed through the kitchen. Delicacies lined the tables, and the cooks, weary and exhausted, scrubbed at the last of the dishes.

"Have you seen Lucas?" I asked.

The head cook shook her head. "No, dearie, he's probably helping his brother prepare for the joust."

I made my way to the courtyard. Outside, squires polished Fredrick's armor and oiled his saddle to a shine. I searched several outbuildings before reaching the armory, where I found Lucas sitting on the floor

staring into a wooden chest. I stood in the doorway and cleared my throat.

Lucas turned around, smiled, and motioned for me to sit next to him. I knelt beside him and looked into the chest. A brilliant suit of armor lay inside, surrounded in fine, navy cloth.

"This was my father's." He stroked the hilt of the sword lying next to the armor.

I clutched his hand. "I know you will become a great knight like your father."

Lucas grinned. "Thank you." A moment of awkward silence passed. "Did you leave because I kissed you?" Lucas finally asked.

"No," I quickly answered. "I really did need some time to figure out who I am." I waited until he meet my gaze before assuring him, "I loved your kiss."

Lucas's lips turned up in a smile. His hand curled around mine. He closed the chest and helped me to my feet.

I paused and gripped Lucas's hand tighter. "Lucas, there is something I need to tell you."

"What is it?" He looked hopeful.

"I do not know how to express it in words." My hands found his cheeks. "So, here." I rose up on my toes and kissed him. It felt so good to stand close to him and feel the warmth of his body. I stepped away and tried to read his expression.

Lucas beamed at me. Without hesitation, Lucas's lips found mine. I relaxed in his arms.

"Whoa ho ho!" The voice sounded like a rumbling canyon, filling the entire space.

Lucas and I tore away from each other.

Fredrick strode toward us. He chuckled and clapped his hands, as if

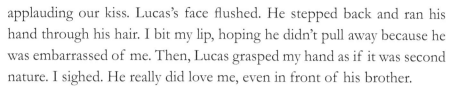

applauding our kiss. Lucas's face flushed. He stepped back and ran his hand through his hair. I bit my lip, hoping he didn't pull away because he was embarrassed of me. Then, Lucas grasped my hand as if it was second nature. I sighed. He really did love me, even in front of his brother.

"I came looking for you, but now, I see you have a good reason to be late." Fredrick winked at me. His dark hair and tanned skin only made his friendly smile brighter.

I reluctantly let go of Lucas's hand. "You better go with Fredrick."

Lucas turned to me. "I'll see you later?" He raised the back of my hand to his lips.

"Indeed." I curtsied and watched the brothers walk toward the arena.

Fredrick playfully punched Lucas in the arm. Lucas laughed and swung back.

I shook my head. Human boys can be so odd.

Lady Hannah's carriage pulled up next to the armory and the door opened. "Hurry, Auriella," she said. "We are going to be late."

I glided into the carriage and sat like a proper lady next to Hannah.

People and animals filled the streets while tents and wagons covered the open fields. Knights, nobles, farmers, mercenaries, and merchants from all over the country came for the festival. The streets bustled with people buying, selling, and trading their wares.

Lady Hannah laced her hands together on her lap. "This is an exciting day for Fredrick. The archbishop is coming, himself, to knight him." Lady Hannah beamed.

"That is wonderful," I replied, paying only partial attention to her as I watched the commotion outside.

We arrived at the crowded arena, where common class and nobility came to enjoy the tournament together. I sat next to Lady Hannah in the

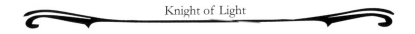

covered viewing stands reserved for the nobles and looked over the arena. The herald introduced each knight into the tournament. Fredrick strode onto the field when he was presented. He was probably the only man alive who could strut fluidly in full armor.

The crowd roared with applause. Fredrick turned to his audience and flipped his sword through the air before handing it to the archbishop. He was always such a showoff.

Fredrick knelt before the bishop. Despite the energized crowd, the archbishop conducted the formal knighting ceremony with reverence and dignity.

Lady Hannah smiled and wiped her tears with a lacey handkerchief. "I wanted him to be knighted in a church, but he wanted his knighting ceremony to be more of a party." Lady Hannah shook her head and continued, "I would have given him an elegant party if he would have been knighted in a church."

I noted the cheering crowd and the line of people at the kegs of ale. Apparently, Fredrick wanted a more boisterous community party instead of a wineglass-tipping-social for nobles only.

After Fredrick's knighting, the tournaments began. I watched Fredrick win his first joust, but I was more interested in watching Lucas and what he did as Fredrick's squire. I savored every move Lucas made, hoping he would search the stands for me.

He focused on the sporting event and didn't seem to notice me. I shifted in my chair, scrunched my eyebrows, and folded my arms.

At the end of the tournament, the archbishop stood and silenced the crowd. A herald in a bright tunic read from a proclamation, "Hear ye, hear ye! Prince Edward has called all men to free the Holy Land from the infidels. Whether ye be of noble birth or common, come, join the prince

this spring on a crusade to the Holy Land and earn your knighthood and your place in Heaven."

I didn't pay much attention to the announcement. I was in too big a rush to find Lucas. The commoners parted a path for me as I raced to the jousting stables where Lucas and Fredrick were.

I entered and curtsied. "Congratulations, gentlemen."

"Look at this." Lucas pointed to a horse and set of armor with a large dent in the breastplate. "Fredrick won these."

Fredrick examined the breastplate. "I will take this to Ruburt and see if he can pound the dent out. It seems Ruburt can do anything with metal."

"And, look what else Fredrick won." Lucas held two swords. "He said we could have them." Lucas grinned. "Would you like to duel tomorrow morning?"

I admired the swords and smirked at Lucas. "Only if you're not worried you'll be beaten by a lady."

Lucas laughed. "We'll just see about that."

I turned to Fredrick. "Thank you, Fre—I mean, Sir Fredrick."

Fredrick flashed me a smile. "You're the first woman to call me 'Sir.' I like the way it sounds coming from a beautiful voice." Lucas scowled at him. Fredrick leaned toward me and whispered loud enough for Lucas to hear. "If my brother ever treats you wrong or behaves unchivalrously, you cut off his ponytail with this sword and come looking for me. I'll treat you right." He glanced at Lucas and laughed.

Lucas's jaw tightened. His eyes narrowed. "Let's go, Auriella." He took my hand and led me out of the arena stables.

We wandered through the festival, looking at the merchants' goods. Lucas examined a piece of leather and asked the tanner, "Can you make

two matching scabbards from this?"

"Yes, m'lord," the tanner replied, taking the leather from Lucas. "I can have them ready tomorrow afternoon."

A familiar odor hit my nose—the smell of blood and sewage mixed with herbs and dirt. I stiffened. My knees felt weak. I jerked my head around, already knowing who I would see. And, there she was. Hazella was arguing with a vendor at a nearby herb stand. Her face was veiled in secrecy by her dark cloak, but there was no doubt it was her.

"Lucas." I grasped his arm. "Don't ask me why, just run." Lucas and I took off at a sprint and sped to the stables at the manor. We raced inside, and I pushed myself into the corner. I wrung my hands, and tried to keep my legs from quivering.

"What's wrong, Auriella?" Lucas asked and slid next to me.

Tears welled in my eyes and streamed down my cheeks. I collapsed onto his shoulder. My heart pounded and my palms grew wet. Lucas wrapped his arms around me. I told him about living with Hazella and the abuse I endured at the witch's hand. I wanted to tell him the rest. I wanted Lucas to know I was the Lady of Neviah, but I held back. I didn't know how Lucas would react. Would he still love me if he knew I wasn't human? Would Lady Hannah still want me as an heir?

"You are a lady now and you are strong." Lucas wiped the tears from my cheeks. "You even look different." Lucas ran his fingers through my hair. "Your skin is clean and beautiful. Your hair has grown back without all the tangles. You are a new person, not the ragamuffin of a lass who came here a year ago. You could walk past Hazella, and she probably wouldn't recognize you."

I nodded—it was true. I was a different person, but seeing the witch brought old feelings of terror. I held my breath. The enemy was close, and

it was only a matter of time before the Shadow Legion found me.

From then on, the sword practicing Lucas and I did became more aggressive. Lucas planned to join the crusades with Prince Edward the following spring, and I had a good reason to learn self-defense skills. As the Lady of Neviah, I would someday face the Shadow Legion.

"Pick up your sword and fight, Auriella," Lucas challenged. His intense gaze held no sign of playfulness.

I tightened my fist and drew my sharpened sword from the scabbard. Our swords clashed and rang with the sound of fierce determination.

There would be no more games. Our carefree childhood was over.

Chapter Twenty-One

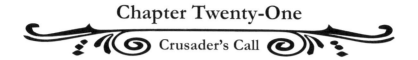

Crusader's Call

I stood in the corner while Lucas and Fredrick buffed their swords. My hands balled into fists. I kicked at the dirt in moody silence. I proposed going with them on the crusade, but the suggestion infuriated Lady Hannah, and even Lucas detested the idea of me going to war.

Out of respect for their wishes, I grudgingly abandoned my plan to stow away on the crusade with them. Lucas and Fredrick would become great knights, and I'd stay in Oswestry.

They finished packing the last of their supplies for the trip to London, where they would join Prince Edward and the rest of the crusaders. Lady Hannah had been in tears the entire week and broke down crying at every family meal. Over the past few weeks, Lucas and I had spent every free moment we could together. We knew it could be months, or years, before we saw each other again.

Lucas placed the last of his supplies in the saddle bag. The realization that he was actually leaving struck me like a punch to the stomach.

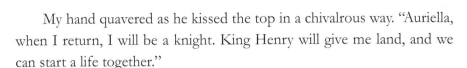

My hand quavered as he kissed the top in a chivalrous way. "Auriella, when I return, I will be a knight. King Henry will give me land, and we can start a life together."

I nodded, blankly. It was a nice dream—if he ever came back. I knew nothing I could say would change his mind. All I could do was lay my head on his shoulder and hold him close. My tears stained the front of his tunic.

"I thought you would be happy for me." Concern overshadowed Lucas's voice.

"I am happy for you." I wiped my cheeks. "I'm just worried that . . . ." His father had died on the last crusade. Lucas was going to the same land to fight the same battles.

"Prince Edward, himself, is leading the crusaders," Lucas tried to comfort me. "My elder brother, Alwaien, promised to look after you while I am away." Lucas lifted my chin, forcing me to meet his eyes. A sly smile formed across his face. "I told Alwaien he would have his hands full."

I let out a fragile laugh to please him, but my heavy heart ached in my chest.

"I promise to come back for you, Lady Auriella." He let go of me. My heart dropped as he stepped back toward his horse.

I couldn't breathe. Every nerve in my body screamed with uncertainty and fear. I mouthed the word "goodbye" and raced for the privacy of the rose garden. I didn't want my unsightly sobbing or losing control and combusting into flames to be Lucas's last memory of me.

I leaned my head against the garden gate and gripped the decorative iron bars. The metal turned red hot in my hands.

Fredrick, who had been hanging back, moved toward Lucas and put his hand on his shoulder. "You love her a lot, don't you?" Fredrick asked.

From the garden, I turned my head to hear them better.

"More than anything." Lucas's voice strained with emotion. I peered through the thick foliage and blossoms.

Fredrick smiled and put his hand on Lucas's shoulder. "You will be a nobler knight than I."

"Why do you say that?" Lucas asked. "You are the kind of knight all men want to be like. I have always admired you. Your laugh could cheer anyone. Not to mention, you are talented, chivalrous, and the maidens swoon over you."

Fredrick mounted his horse. "I became a knight for glory. You will become a knight for love."

Lucas swung onto his horse and pulled back on the reins. "Brother, there is no other man I would want to fight beside." The horses kicked up the dusty road as they rounded the bend and disappeared.

I released my grip on the gate and sunk to my knees. The disfigured iron sweltered in the shape of my clenched fingers.

Spring and summer passed. The Harvest Festival wasn't the same without Lucas. There were rumors that I was the most sought-after of all the eligible women in the providence. Well, just because Lucas had been away for six months didn't make me eligible. I refused to join in the festivities as they only brought anger and emptiness. Instead, I practiced fighting in an empty field where only the scarecrows could gawk at me.

I whirled a broad sword over my head. Using this heavier weapon toned my arms and made me quicker with lighter weapons. I danced with the weapon as the blade whistled through the air.

A trail of dust billowed into the sky as two riders galloped toward me. It was Lord Broian and Master Keladron. I rolled my eyes. They came toward the gate and Broian flashed me an over-confident smile. I

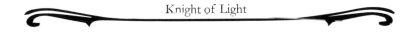

pretended not to notice. I swung into a defensive position before severing the head of the nearest scarecrow.

From the corner of my eye, I saw the two suitors galloping away in the other direction. I hoped they would spread the word that I was not so eligible after all.

Winter hit hard and was bitterly cold without Lucas's warm hand curled around mine. I engrossed myself in the geography books, reading about the places Lucas would visit in the Middle East.

Spring came again, and I refused to celebrate my seventeenth birthday. I wouldn't celebrate anything until Lucas returned.

I continued to push my body to the limits, strengthening my muscles and quickening my attack so I would still be Lucas's equal when he returned from war.

I volunteered to help Ruburt by hauling loads of firewood and farm equipment. My feet toughened, and my thighs toned as I raced Cassi through the woods every morning.

I rode my midnight black horse through the meadow while the wind tousled my long hair like scarlet streamers in a windstorm. I dismounted by the rose garden gate and stared down the dirt road, hoping to see Lucas riding home. I daydreamed about our wedding day and envisioned Lucas standing with me in the cathedral. A breeze from the rose garden danced through the air and painted my hair with the romantic scent. I imagined the manor decorated in roses, Lady Hannah beaming proudly, and Lucas in a royal knight's tunic.

I waited by the gate until nightfall enveloped Oswestry, then trudged to the manor for dinner. Alwaien and Lady Hannah enjoyed a conversation while I pushed the food around my plate and thought about Lucas.

"My lady," one of the servants interrupted the conversation. The

servant held up an ivory parchment. "A letter from the crusades."

Lady Hannah and I jumped from our chairs. Finally, a letter from Lucas and Fredrick. "Read it out loud," I begged.

Lady Hannah smiled and broke the seal. "Dear Lord and Lady . . . ." Lady Hannah furrowed her brow and continued to read silently.

I wrung my hands. Why was the letter addressed so formally?

Lady Hannah collapsed to the floor and buried her face in her hands. Alwaien and I rushed to her side.

"What? What is it?" I asked.

She handed the letter to me and turned into Alwaien's shoulder, sobbing.

I skimmed over the letter. My legs lost their strength. I slipped against the wall and dropped to the ground. A tight lump formed in my throat. I felt myself suffocating and blinked past the tears to read the letter again. Six words stood out as if written in bold:

Crusade failed, Fredrick and Lucas SLAIN.

There must be a mistake. I felt a scream rising in my throat and fought to keep it from escaping. I checked the address on letter, hoping against hope that the letter had been meant for someone else. It just couldn't be true.

A few maids rushed to me, but I held up my hand, signaling to them to keep their distance. I read it again before tossing the letter aside. I stood and raced to the stables where Lucas and I had spent so much time together and flung myself onto a pile of cold straw.

"No! This can't be." I released the scream I'd been holding.

My angry face burned with tears. Neviahan flames ran up my arms. My heart hurt so bad that I couldn't move, but I had to get up before I set the barn ablaze. It took all my strength to stand and stumble to the

horses' trough. I laid my flaming body into the filthy water. The horses' cold water soaked my clothes and hair, extinguishing the fire and diluting my salty tears. "Please, no. It can't be true." I sobbed.

I cried until I was numb. I could barely see through my swollen eyes as I stumbled like a drunk back to the manor, hoping it was all a nightmare.

It seemed as if a dark cloud hung over the manor. The days and nights blended together as the days were dark and the nights were sleepless.

Lady Hannah shut herself in her room and refused comfort and nourishment. Two days later she called for me and her last son, Alwaien. When we entered the room, Lady Hannah held out her hand toward her son, but she struggled to breathe his name. Alwaien rushed to her side while I stood at the foot of the bed, feeling like an empty shell. I hardly recognized her. White hair hung in wispy thin strands around her face. A yellow tinge covered Lady Hannah's skin and age spots dotted her like a plague.

Although her breath rasped weakly, her words were earnest. "I have lived a long time—a good deal longer than most people do. A mother should never outlive her children." She coughed and added, "I am giving you each half of the estate." Hannah paused, and focused on Alwaien. "Take care of Auriella."

I tensed at her request.

"Oh, Mother, I will." Alwaien glanced at me and choked back a sob of his own. "I will."

"Auriella," Hannah whispered. I stared at Lady Hannah, unable to move. Alwaien grasped my hand and pulled me over to stand next to his mother. Lady Hannah handed the ruby necklace to me. "Thank you. It truly was a precious gift, but the longer I keep it, the more it becomes a curse. I can't continue to live and watch everyone around me die."

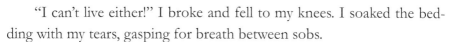

"I can't live either!" I broke and fell to my knees. I soaked the bedding with my tears, gasping for breath between sobs.

"Auriella, look at me."

I wiped my wet face. My emotions were heightened. The fire scorched me inside. I forced myself to breathe deeply, suppressing the flames.

Hannah's eyes filled with white light. She grasped my hand with amazing strength. Her words struck with a fierce and powerful edge. "Auriella, you must live!"

Lady Hannah fell onto her pillow. Her lifeless eyes rolled behind her heavy lids. Alwaien reached up and closed his mother's eyelids over her lifeless stare.

I stood and backed away. This couldn't be happening. I stared at the necklace in my hands. Hannah's last plea—you must live—resonated in my mind and shook me to the core. Alwaien embraced me. I crumpled into his arms. The heavy necklace slipped from my fingers and echoed off the stone floor.

A priest came the next morning, and by that afternoon, I was standing outside in the rain, staring down into the pit where Alwaien and a few of our manor servants lowered Hannah's coffin.

I had no more tears to cry as the rain soaked through the fine black cloth of my gown. My body and mind were numb from having so much tragedy seize me. A ruby rose slipped from my fingertips into the cold earth.

The next morning, I left the manor while it was still dark outside. I rode my horse to the top of a nearby hill and watched the sunrise, as Lucas and I had done many times. Not wanting to be consoled, I returned home in the evening when I hoped everyone would be sleeping. I climbed the trellis to my balcony, entered the room, and flung my cape onto the bed.

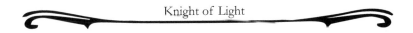

"Where were you?"

Hearing a man's voice, I whirled around. It was only Alwaien, sitting in the corner on a lounge chair. "Riding!" I snapped. "Why are you in my room?"

"Auriella, where have you been riding?" Alwaien stood and advanced toward me.

"It does not matter," I answered coldly.

"Auriella, you are the lady of the estate now. You have duties in the manor. We see you riding off in the morning, but no one has spoken with you for days. We have all been worried."

"I can take care of myself." I sat on the edge of my bed and unlaced my riding boots. I glanced at him from the corner of my eye. He still wasn't leaving.

Alwaien came closer and dropped the ruby necklace in my hand. I stared at the large, blood-red stone before closing my fist around it.

"Auriella, mother told me on her deathbed, she wanted me to take care of you." He reached for my hand. "I wish for your concurrence in marriage. We can rule our estates together instead of splitting Oswestry . . . Lucas would have wanted it this way."

I yanked my hand away and clenched the bedpost. I narrowed my eyes and tossed the necklace onto the pillow. "How do you know what Lucas would have wanted? I knew him better than anyone else!" I paused and drew my arm across my face, refusing to let tears fall. "I knew his deepest wish, his strengths, and all his weaknesses!"

Alwaien's face turned into a crimson scowl, but I continued, "Are you infuriated because Lady Hannah granted half of the inheritance to me? Is that why you want to wed me, so you can take it all?"

Alwaien's hand shot out wickedly and struck me across the face.

I retaliated and swung at his jaw with a hard fist backed by all my pain and anger. Alwaien fell to the floor and stared at me with wide eyes.

"Get out!" I yelled at him. He scrambled to his feet, holding his jaw. "Get out!" I pointed to the door. "You can have the estate!" Alwaien left, closing the door behind him. I dropped to the ground and whimpered, "I just want my happy life back."

My happy life wasn't coming back, and Oswestry held too many painful memories I needed to bury. I had to start over and I knew I couldn't do that here in Oswestry. I needed to escape to someplace new.

I dressed in clothes of solid black. Jacquine had reluctantly made the dark, men's clothes for me months ago when I had thought about joining the crusade in disguise. With my sword strapped to my side, I flung a traveling cloak around my shoulders.

I navigated the halls of the manor for the last time and knocked on Ruburt's door. I pulled the hood over my head to hide my puffy eyes.

Ruburt opened the door. He looked surprised to see me. "Auriella, come in."

I shook my head. I was glad Cassi was with him so I didn't need to explain this twice. I glanced down at the rainbow ring on my finger. "I am leaving tonight." I tried to keep my voice sure. "I can't ask you to leave Oswestry, but—"

"Of course we'll come with you," Ruburt broke in. "Besides, who'll protect you from the wolves?"

"Or fairies?" Cassi added.

I smiled. I didn't need their protection, but I needed good friends who would understand.

I waited while Ruburt and Cassi gathered their things, watching carefully to make sure we weren't discovered. The last thing I wanted was to have someone try to stop us from leaving. Along with our personal belongings, we discreetly packed a few necessary supplies from the kitchen. One at a time, we walked across the courtyard to the barn, where I quietly saddled my horse while Ruburt saddled his pony. Just as the moon showed its crest over the treetops, Ruburt, Cassi, and I rode off into the night, leaving Oswestry behind. I wasn't running away. I definitely had a direction in mind. I didn't know how, but I would find a way to become a knight and complete Lucas's dream.

Chapter Twenty-Two

Mercenaries

At noon, the sound of wagon wheels rolled on the road nearby. I arose from my earthy bed of grass and noticed the travelers' heavy armor and wagons full of weapons and supplies.

"Mercenaries," I whispered and nudged Ruburt awake. "They are successful warriors and will know how I can become a knight."

We followed them for several hours before they stopped at a clearing in the woods. The soldiers sang songs and whistled as they set up tents and prepared dinner. Ruburt told me to watch them from the forest, but my curiosity got the better of me. I stowed into their camp like a stealthy predator and scurried up a sturdy tree to listen to their heroic stories.

"Once in my travels," a giant of a man spoke, "after a long day of journeying, we set camp for the night," he continued as he strode toward the tree where I hid. "The fire was a-dying, and we were about to retire to our tents . . . when," his voice lowered to a whisper. I leaned closer to hear, my skin tingled in suspense. "They ambushed us from the trees!" He

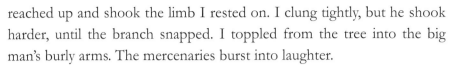

reached up and shook the limb I rested on. I clung tightly, but he shook harder, until the branch snapped. I toppled from the tree into the big man's burly arms. The mercenaries burst into laughter.

The big man chuckled. "What are you doing in the tree, wee one?"

"Let go of me!" I wiggled out of his arms then stood as tall as I could. In my most regal voice, I announced, "I have been assessing you travelers for the quality of attack and defense skills you command."

The men erupted with laughter. I felt myself turn a shade of red.

The big man snorted. "Why will you have interest in this, lassie?"

Without thinking, I answered, "I thought I'd join your band of men and someday become a knight."

My fists clenched as the mercenaries rolled with laughter.

Ruburt charged into camp with his dagger brandished. "Do you have any idea who this lady is?"

The men of the camp broke into a chorus of laughter once again. One of them pointed to Ruburt. "The knight's squire!"

Ruburt dismounted and advanced. I gripped his shoulder and pulled him back as the mercenaries drew their swords. "Let me at 'em!" Ruburt shouted.

"You better put that toothpick away, little man, before you hurt yourself," one of the mercenaries patronized.

"Please, put it away," I whispered under my breath.

Cassi tugged on Ruburt's beard where she was hiding. "Ruburt be like pixie to them." Ruburt paused and eyed the men before putting his dagger into its scabbard. He crossed his arms and scowled.

Maybe this was a bad idea after all. I would find another way to become a knight if the mercenaries wouldn't help me.

"All right, lassie. We can see you and your squire have heart. We

can teach you how to become a proper knight," the biggest man gasped between laughs. "But ye'll need to prove yourself before joining our group of mercenaries."

"How do I do that?" I asked.

"You will need to best one of us in a duel."

The mercenaries looked like giants, and their years of military experience showed. I felt like a child standing next to them, and I probably looked like an easy target. I twitched against a smile. Wouldn't they be surprised? With modesty and false innocence, I agreed to the duel.

"My name's Philip," the big man said. "What's your name, lass?"

"Auriella." I innately held out my hand for him to kiss the top. He grabbed my hand and shook it with a firm grip.

"Is there more to your name?" Philip asked.

"Auriella, that is all," I answered curtly. I wasn't about to tell him I was actually Lady Auriella of Oswestry.

I thought he was just going to make fun of me again, or at least tell me that I couldn't become a knight. Instead, he asked, "Very well, Auriella, why do you want to become a knight?"

I stared down at the rainbow ring on my sparkling hand. The truth was painful, but I couldn't think of a better reason. "My fiancé, went on the crusade with Prince Edward a year ago, but was slain in battle." My eyes grew hot with tears, but I held them back. I couldn't let Philip think I was an overly emotional woman. I forced a smile on my face and said, "He taught me how to sword fight." I hoped to change the subject to my weapon skills. If I wanted to lament and discuss Lucas, I would have stayed at the manor.

"Well then." Philip stepped back and motioned to the sword at my side. "You know how to use this? Let's see if you canst best me with that

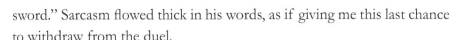

sword." Sarcasm flowed thick in his words, as if giving me this last chance to withdraw from the duel.

There was no way I was backing down now. I pointed to my staff, which Ruburt retrieved from the few supplies we packed. "I will use this. My sword is sharp, and I don't want to hurt you too badly," I said in a strong, sure voice.

"That's big talk coming from a small lady. Very well," he said with a hint of playful mockery. "Let's see if you canst best me or anyone with that stick."

Philip slammed his sword on a long branch and hacked it from a tree. "What are you doing?" I asked.

He trimmed the smaller limbs from the branch. "I'm making a staff." I furrowed my brow. "Why?"

"Only a coward would use a sword to fight a woman armed with only a staff. If we're going to fight, it'll be on equal grounds." An effortless smile beamed across his face.

I narrowed my eyes and hoped this didn't mean he was going to go easy on me. If he did, I would hit him harder.

"Your staff is crooked," I bantered. "Maybe you should have chosen a straighter branch to make your staff out of."

Philip shook his head and chuckled darkly. "Nah. This staff will leave a nice twisted welt across your backside."

I smirked. This was going to be fun.

Ruburt turned to me. "Don't use any fancy moves," he advised. "Just move in quick and take the victory."

"Cassi see giant man fall like ant," Cassi whispered from Ruburt's beard. She squished her hands together for effect.

The mercenaries stood in a large circle, every man an arm's length

from the next. Philip and I circled a couple of times, testing each other's reflexes by tapping our weapons. I eyed him. He was huge, muscular, and bulky. If nothing else, his appearance was intimidating.

I evaluated Philip's dark brown eyes; they were friendly, but intent on winning. His scowl caused lines to form across his forehead. I smiled back angelically. Philip inched closer, towering over me, then attacked.

I blocked his assault and struck back, aiming for his face with the point of my staff like a spear. I stayed light on my feet and watched the flicks of his wrists.

Philip was well-trained and would be less likely to make a mistake in his attack or defense. I blocked another strike, but the blow on my staff knocked me to the ground. He lunged to finish the duel. I skillfully rolled on my back, somersaulted, and sprang to my feet. Philip swung at my knees. I leapt over his staff, and, as he overextended, I intuitively whacked him between the shoulder blades.

"Your agility is amazing." He huffed, wiped the sweat dewing on his brow, and rolled his shoulders.

"Thank you. I wish I had your strength."

He started to tire and became clumsy. He was big and strong, but moved slower and didn't get his swings in as fast. It seemed he was used to relying on his size and strength to quickly win a match. I hit him on the stomach and then on the back of his legs. Philip fell to his knees and dropped his staff. I whirled behind him, thrust my staff across his throat, and squeezed. His big arms swung around the staff and tried to pull me off.

The men whispered on the side-lines. "Philip has never lost a match before."

"It appears the lass is beating him."

"Nah, Philip's going easy on her."

Philip's huge hands grabbed my staff. He pulled the weapon away from his throat with ferocious strength. I released the chokehold and twisted away to confront him as he rose to his feet.

Philip's petulant gaze fixed on me. "No one makes a fool of me in front of my men." He clenched his teeth together and growled like a bear. I kept my eyes on him and backed toward the edge of the circle of men under a tree. "Wanna fight rough? Do you, lass?" Philip narrowed his eyes and clenched his jaw. He gripped his crooked staff and swung at me again and again as I retreated. He swung at my feet. I leapt over the weapon, spun around him, swatted his legs, and knocked him to the ground once again.

Like a mad bull, he tossed the staff at me and charged in an attempt to grab and wrestle me to the ground. I flipped into a back handspring and, with my momentum, jumped and grasped a tree branch above me. I pulled my dangling legs out of the way as Philip charged into the two men standing behind me. His force continued to carry him headlong into the tree trunk, knocking him out cold.

The men of the camp were silent, their mouths and eyes wide in astonishment. They examined their leader, who was now lying unconscious next to the tree. One of the men retrieved a bucket of cold water and dumped it over Philip's head.

My intention had not been to knock him out, just wear him down until he surrendered.

I wrung my hands together until Philip awoke from his tree encounter, wet and gasping for air. He stood and steadied himself on the tree. "That girl tricked me," he muttered and pointed his finger at me.

Once Philip regained his balance, he stomped to me, glaring. Water

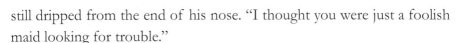

still dripped from the end of his nose. "I thought you were just a foolish maid looking for trouble."

I was about to drop my staff and run, but his terrifying scowl faded and a huge grin spread tight across his face. "You are an excellent challenger, and you hit like a man!"

I wasn't expecting that at all. I smiled sheepishly. "Er . . . Thank you?"

"Maybe you can teach my men a thing or two. Welcome to our band." Philip gave me a suffocating bear hug. He set me down like a flimsy doll and asked in a joking tone, "Best out of three?"

Chapter Twenty-Three

London

Throughout the summer and into autumn, the mercenaries traveled all over the country. Philip took me as his apprentice, an honor the men said was bestowed to only a few. I learned new skills, such as archery on horseback, tactics for defending against groups, and fighting men with shields. Not only did Philip help me refine my skills, but he taught me how to run a mercenary business.

My literacy and etiquette aided in negotiations for the mercenary band's contractual employment. Wealthy landlords were always looking for freelance military help.

Our next stop was London. This would be a perfect place to purchase supplies and earn money as an independent army.

Near sunset, we rode over the emerald hills toward London. A large stone castle towered above a sea of beautiful thatched roofs and mortar homes. Smoke trickled from the cottage chimneys as twilight approached. A few of the first stars appeared in the indigo sky and mirrored the lights

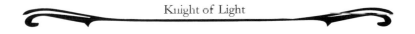

of the city. The only thing that could have made this moment more splendid was to have Lucas riding at my side.

We set camp on the outskirts London, and Philip went into the city to scout for business opportunities. It was almost midnight before he returned. He tied his horse to a tree and stood next to the fire. The men all looked as anxious as I felt. We were running out of money and needed to find work.

Philip kicked at the dirt and stuck his hands in his pockets. This couldn't be good news. "I have spoken to several of the innkeepers . . .." He wagged his head, drawing out the suspense. "And, it looks like this city has lots of trouble." A smile flared across his face. The men cheered, and I let out a sigh of relief. Lots of trouble meant job security. "In the morning I will assign each of you to new posts, except for you, Auriella."

I narrowed my eyes and rose to my feet. "Except for me? Why can't I help? I'm just as good of a fighter as anyone here. I can do the job." Philip's eyes saddened. He looked to the ground. His pained and ambivalent expression stabbed at me. I balled my hands into fists. "Philip! You know I can do the job." I didn't hide the hurt in my voice. Why was he holding me back?

Philip took a lamp and motioned for me to follow so we could speak privately. We walked until we were near the woods. I folded my arms under my chest and shrugged away when he tried to put a comforting hand on my shoulder.

"Philip, I'm not going to take 'no' for an answer. I'm going to help, whether you like it or not."

"Maybe this will change your mind." Philip reached into his vest and handed me a rolled parchment.

I tightened my jaw and took the parchment. "What's this?"

"Open it and see." He leaned against a large tree and smirked like he was about to laugh. This must be one of his jokes. I unrolled the parchment. It looked official and the seal on the bottom was authentic.

Hear ye, hear ye! By order of King Henry the Third, the kingdom has a shortage of knights to protect England. Therefore, King Henry invites all able-bodied men to apply for knighthood.

Signed,
The Captain of the Royal Army

Philip laughed and waved one hand in front of my face. "Auriella, wake up, lass."

I read it again before responding. "I . . . I." I tried to regain composure, though I felt like screaming for joy. I wanted to charge into the castle that moment and start testing to become a royal knight.

Philip put his arm around me and pulled me into a bear hug. "Here's your chance to become a knight."

He set me on my feet. I clasped my hands and bounced. "Yes, yes, yes!" I grabbed his hands and spun with him in a circle. "This is a dream come true."

Philip laughed, and then noticed the men watching us from a distance. He regained his rugged, stern composure and forced a cough. "Tomorrow we will go into town and get you some armor."

The next morning, Philip escorted me into the city. There were so many people and a shop for everything. It was like the Harvest Festival every day. I could've spent so much money there. I gripped my purse tight and focused on the armor smith's shop ahead.

Philip opened the door for me. The air in the shop hung thick with ash. Orange flames lit the room and reflected off tools and metal scraps.

"Ehem . . . ." Philip cleared his throat over the sound of clanking

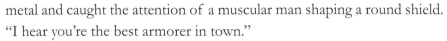

metal and caught the attention of a muscular man shaping a round shield. "I hear you're the best armorer in town."

The armorer looked up and eyed us with his one good eye. "Aye, for a price, I am." He wiped his sooty hands on his already soiled shop apron. He glared at me and looked offended by my presence.

I shifted my weight and averted my attention to the works in progress around the shop. Maybe he was too busy to help us. His unsettling glances stabbed at me. Something was wrong. He acted like he hated me, and he didn't even know who I was or why I was there. I squirmed inside and casually half-turned behind Philip's bulky frame.

"I need you to fit some armor for the lady here." Philip pointed at me. I inwardly cringed. Now all the attention was on me, and it wasn't good.

The armorer wrinkled his leathery face. "For her?"

Philip nodded.

"You can't be serious," he argued. "She looks like a girl, not a knight. Take her to a dress shop." He spat on the ground and turned to his work.

Philip leaned forward, snatched the man by the back of his shirt and whirled him around. I had never seen Philip so angry. Even the muscular armorer looked intimidated. Philip's crimson face pulsed above his strained neck, but he spoke calmly. "You're right. She is a girl, and the best warrior I've ever trained. She's quick and agile and can spill all your organs before you can draw your sword. I need you to make armor tailored for that kind of warrior."

I repeated his words in my mind. Me, a warrior? The best he's ever trained. A smile pulled across my face, but I tried to stay firm and regal like a soldier. After all, I had to keep a good appearance for Philip's reputation.

Philip released the armorer, pulled a pouch from his tunic, and

dropped it on the table. The unmistakable sound of coins clinked inside. "No, Philip." I reached for my purse.

Philip put his hand up. "I insist. It's an honor for a father to purchase his son's first set of armor. I know you're not my son . . . or daughter, but you don't have a father, and I never had a son. Please, allow me this privilege."

"I . . . I don't know what to say." I dropped my shoulders.

"Say ye'll show those pretty noble boys how real men fight."

I beamed mischievously. "Yes, Sir!"

The armorer opened the pouch and looked inside. He counted the coins and said, "Fine, I will make armor for the lady."

Philip turned back to the armorer and jerked him closer. "Are you married?" he asked.

"Yes," the armorer replied in a hesitant tone.

"That's a surprise—poor lass." Philip shook his head. "Imagine me coming after your wife with a sword."

The armorer knocked Philip's hand away. "Are you threatening me?"

"Of course not." Philip feigned innocence. "But I want you to make Auriella a suit of armor you would feel comfortable having your wife wear if she had to face me in battle."

"I only make the best," the armorer replied. "I'll have it done in two weeks."

As promised, two weeks later, the armor was ready, and it really was the best armor I had ever seen. The craftsmanship was second to none. Cassi purred with excitement, while Ruburt helped me pack the last of our belongings.

I looked to the castle. Tonight I was going to be dining with knights and royalty in the palace. If I worked hard enough I could be knighted by my next birthday. I took the proclamation scroll from my pack and read the words, just as I had many times the previous night. This time I saw something I hadn't noticed until now. "Oh, no!"

Ruburt took the scroll from me, his eyes scanned the page. "What's wrong?"

"Don't you see? It calls for 'All able-bodied men.' Men! I am not a man. When I ride to the castle, they will turn me away as soon as they see me." I recalled the way the armorer reacted to me. Obviously the idea of a female fighter offended him. Lady Hannah hadn't even like the idea of me fighting in battle. What if this prevented me from being knighted?

Ruburt's eyes opened wide and he read the parchment again. "Well, I, uh . . .," he stammered. "This'll make things difficult."

I closed my hands into fists and stared at the high castle in the center of the city. "We've got to create a plan. Maybe if we explain things to them . . .."

Ruburt shook his head. "Explain to the captain of the guard? He has a reputation for being a tyrant and hosts a beheading once a month."

I dropped my head and exhaled the breath I was holding. There had to be a way. This was so unfair.

Cassi's eyes opened wide. "Cassi know! Cassi show!"

I looked up, but had little hope Cassi actually had an idea that would get me knighted.

Ruburt rolled the scroll and handed it to me. "Cassi, this better be a good plan."

Chapter Twenty-Four

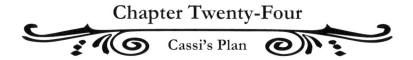

Cassi's Plan

The mid-morning light gleamed off the new armor like jewels as I rode toward the gates of London. Inside the metal shell, sweat beaded on my brow and trickled down my neck. Wearing full armor in the sun felt like roasting in an oven, but at least it offered a convincing disguise.

The pixie and dwarf hid under my billowing cape. I led Ruburt's small horse beside my own mare and feebly hoped it would pass as a packhorse. We approached the first guarded gate of the city. I clutched the scroll with the call for knights in my fist.

"Halt!" one of the guards called out. "Who art thou and what is thy business in this city?"

From under my cape, Ruburt spoke in his deep voice, "My name is Bronson. I have come to answer the king's call for knights."

Bronson, I thought. Where was he getting that name from? I would have chosen a more romantic name like Gladimer or Nathanial.

The guard gave me a suspicious look. "Where do you hail from?"

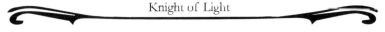

My heart raced. No one was going to believe this disguise. They might as well behead me now.

"I'm a pure Englishman through and through and will hail from wherever the king sends me," Ruburt said.

That was a pretty good answer. I gestured with my hands and drew the guard's attention to the scroll with the proclamation on it.

"You may pass. Report to the captain of the guards."

Cassi started to giggle as we rode into the city. Even Ruburt chuckled from under my cape. "If knighthood doesn't work out for you, Auriella, maybe you can become an actor," Ruburt teased.

I wrinkled my nose. "A woman actor—how inappropriate." In theater, if a woman's role was needed, a young boy played the part. Young men who aspired to become actors were initiated in the performance community by strapping on corsets and prancing around like women until their whiskers came in and ruined their soft baby faces.

"And you see nothing wrong with a woman becoming a knight?" Ruburt let out a surrendering sigh. "I swear, I'll never figure you out, Auriella."

I wasn't sure what he meant, but I wasn't going to make a fool of myself. We rode through the merchant district and passed the elaborate homes of those who could afford to live within the protective walls of the city. It looked like Cassi's plan was going to work—at least for now.

Under the cape, Cassi wiggled back and forth, trying to see all the people. Her wings tickled Ruburt's nose as she fidgeted, and he let out a tremendous string of sneezes. A passerby called, "God bless thee!"

Ruburt swatted at the pixie in annoyance. "I think I'm allergic to pixie dust."

We passed the execution stage. My stomach twisted. What if we were

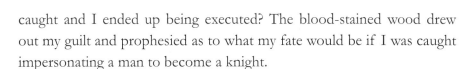

caught and I ended up being executed? The blood-stained wood drew out my guilt and prophesied as to what my fate would be if I was caught impersonating a man to become a knight.

I slowed the horse. It wasn't too late to turn back. My heart pounded against ribs. What would Lucas do?

I knew exactly what Lucas would do. He would serve his country, even if that meant giving his life.

I urged my horse forward, and I made sure my helmet covered my face. In the courtyard, a tall man draped in a crimson and black uniform held his helmet at his side with one hand. A gold shield was embroidered on his tunic. This had to be the captain. He looked just as fierce as Ruburt had described him. His seasoned face was lined in a way that made him look permanently irritated by everyone and everything around him.

I whispered to Ruburt, "When I stop, I will be in front of the captain. I need you to ask him where we are to go." Ruburt nodded. I rode toward the captain and halted a short distance from him. I lifted the visor of my helmet and saluted. I might have been overly paranoid, but I squinted to make my large, almond-shape eyes seem less feminine.

"I understand you are the captain of the guards?" Ruburt's voice questioned.

The captain turned toward me and replied, "I am he."

"I am Bronson. I have come in response to the call for knights," Ruburt said from under my cape, and I tilted my head and nodded as if it was me speaking.

The captain rolled his eyes and motioned for a couple of squires to assist me in dismounting. Before they reached me, Ruburt swung from the horse and held out his hand to help me down. The squires stepped back and looked startled before they snickered at the dwarf.

"Be on with your work!" The captain scowled and turned toward me. "I see you have brought a small squire."

Ruburt and I both opened our mouths, but hesitated. If either one of us spoke, the captain would know we tried to trick him and there would be a double beheading.

The captain waved his hand. "Never mind. With the short supply of men these days, even a dwarf is needed as an assistant." Ruburt and I looked at each other. "You, Bronson, have your small squire get your things and follow me."

Ruburt and I gathered our belongings and followed the captain through an arched doorway into the castle. Ruburt swatted at his beard, obviously trying to get Cassi to hold still. I said a prayer in my heart that this would work. We followed the captain up a stone staircase and came to a halt in front of an open door. The walls were stone and devoid of decoration except for a single torch in one corner above a wooden bench.

"Here is a changing room," the captain said. "We dine at sunset. A bell will ring six times to call everyone to the dining hall. Change out of your armor, get cleaned, and come in dinner apparel." He pointed to a set of clothing laid out on the bench. "This is the tunic for the candidates who wish to become royal knights. You will need to wear this when walking around the castle and grounds." The tunic looked like the one the captain wore, with the exception of the gold trim. A green belt lay in a pile next to the tunic.

The captain pointed down the hallway. "Take your armor to the armory where it will be stored. You will be assigned a place to sleep after dinner." The captain scowled at me. "Do you understand?"

I nodded.

"Good," the captain stated. His black leather boots clicked against

the stone floor as he marched back to the courtyard.

Ruburt helped me out of my armor, and I went into the dressing room. I pulled several shirts from my pack and bulked up to hide my feminine frame before tossing on the uniform. I braided my hair and stuffed it in my chainmail hood. I flung a cloak around my shoulders, and then pulled the hood of my cloak over my head as well.

I opened the door and strutted out into the hall. I puffed out my chest and flexed my muscles. I threw Ruburt a debonair smile and dropped my voice to a low growl. "Do I look like a man?"

Ruburt raised his eyebrow and cringed like he had swallowed something bitter.

I slumped. "Come on, we can't have you hiding under my cape speaking for me at dinner. If young men can play the part of women in theater, then why can't a woman play the part of a young man?"

Ruburt shook his head. "I can't believe you're going through with this." I narrowed my eyes and Ruburt put up his hands like he was surrendering under my glare. "Just don't talk to anyone and you'll be fine."

Six chimes echoed through the castle, indicating it was time for dinner. We entered the dining room and found it full of young men recounting tales and bragging about their skills. Most of the young men were sons from noble families. I hoped I wouldn't run into anyone I had known while I was in Oswestry. I tried to avoid conversation, but a man approached me. He looked so young; he probably couldn't even shave yet.

"So, you are competing for a place in the guard?" he asked in a friendly tone.

I nodded.

"We are in the same barrack," he said.

Panic washed over me. Same barrack? I wasn't getting my own private

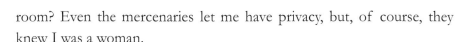

room? Even the mercenaries let me have privacy, but, of course, they knew I was a woman.

He continued, "I can tell by the color of your belt." I glanced at my green belt then around the room. All the trainees wore one of three colored belts: blue, green, and red. "Some of us are practicing tomorrow morning before the big competition. Would you like to join us?"

I only heard part of what he said, but nodded.

"Is this your squire?"

Ruburt growled in his deep voice. "Do you have a problem with that?" Ruburt sounded intimidating, even for a dwarf.

The young man hesitated. "At least you have a squire. Most of us came on our own. I was a squire when I arrived, but I'm going to leave a knight."

I let out a soft smile. He was so adorable. I wished I could adopt him as my little brother.

Some other men advanced toward us. I stiffened. They handed the boy a large glass of wine and pulled him away.

"Well, good luck," he called back.

"That was close," I whispered to Ruburt.

"It'll get worse, trust me," he grumbled.

I ate my meal while watching the men get drunker. Men are such barbarians when they think women aren't around. I tugged on Ruburt's sleeve. "Let's get out of here."

I retired to the barrack with the green stripe above the doorway. My heart sunk and my stomach twisted until I felt sick. A dozen men occupied the room. They danced and roughhoused in a drunken stupor. More entered the room. This just kept getting worse. I skittered toward the two vacant cots in the corner of the room and covered myself with the wool

blanket provided. I was just going to lay here and pretend to be asleep so everyone would leave me alone. Ruburt sat on the cot next to mine. I stared at the rainbow ring on my hand. Maybe this was a bad idea after all. I thought it would be exciting to have a secret identity, but instead, it was more of an inconvenience.

I rolled over, turning my back to them, and eventually, fell asleep. When I awoke, all of my unwanted roommates lay passed out in heavy sleep. Wine soaked the ground like blood. These young men, who hoped to become knights, would no doubt have nasty headaches when they awoke.

Right now I had a bigger problem.

"Cassi," I whispered. Cassi stirred awake and crawled out of Ruburt's beard. "We have to come up with a better disguise or I will be executed before I get a chance to serve my country. What can we do?" I asked Cassi because she would never suggest that I cut my hair or learn to belch on command.

Cassi thought for a moment. Her tired eyes brightened with an idea. She clutched her fairy wand and snickered at Ruburt who still slept beside us. "Auriella needs fairy magic. Just wait and see what Cassi do to Ruburt." She laughed.

Hopefully, Ruburt would forgive us.

Chapter Twenty-Five

First Test

The young men of my barrack marched down the hallway to the trial grounds. Almost all of them had hangovers and couldn't walk in a straight line, let alone in unison. I prayed we would be tested individually and not as a whole group or I would have no chance of winning this competition against the blue and red teams.

Once we reached the arena, the crowd cheered wildly. King Henry sat with the captain in the front row. From the stands, Ruburt waved gruffly. I smiled and waved back. He must have found out about Cassi switching our voices. I had tried to convince Cassi to give me Ruburt's beard as well, but the pixie utterly refused to make me ugly, even if it would have made Ruburt prettier.

I glanced across the arena at my competitors. Every one of them looked alert and ready for a fight. I assessed them and their weapons as the captain explained the rules of the competition. Two men would enter the arena and duel for the duration of the hourglass, which was about

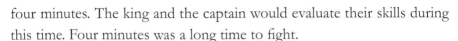

four minutes. The king and the captain would evaluate their skills during this time. Four minutes was a long time to fight.

I waited as, one by one, the men from my group were called for their duels. I wished I could have been first, just to get my duel over with. I chewed on my nails. Lady Hannah always scolded me for biting my pretty nails when I was nervous, but I didn't need pretty nails now.

The herald called the man before me. The contestants behind me sat, hunched over or leaned against the wall for support. Sweat beaded on their foreheads, above their glazed eyes. At least I stood a chance in this fight. So far, no one from my barrack had won their duel. After four minutes, the guard at the gate motioned for me. I took a deep breath, gripped my sword, and stepped into the arena.

I felt pretty good about this fight, until my competitor entered the arena. He was twice my size, in weight, and a good foot and a half taller. He laughed, and his voice sounded like thunder. I forced myself to stay relaxed and ignore his taunting. If I could beat Philip then I could beat him.

"Kneel when ready," the captain commanded.

My competitor knelt impatiently in the center of the arena.

I mechanically saluted the king and captain and then knelt beside my competitor. The king motioned for us to arise and said, "Begin!"

My competitor immediately forced me on the defensive before I could get a proper stance. He swung his sword hard, but was careful to stay in control.

I parried and waited for him to slip up and leave an opening for me to reach in and disable him. I blocked his blow, forcing him to overextend. The tip of my sword shot up and knocked the helmet off his head. He looked stunned, as he blinked his eyes and shook his head like he was

trying to shake off my attack.

Black blood oozed like tar from a cut on his chin where my initial strike hit. His lips quivered and his teeth gnashed together. He wiped the shadowy blood from his chin and licked it off his fingers. How repulsive! I forced down a gag. Why did his blood look so different? The veins in his neck bulged as he struck again with more intensity.

I rebounded and aimed for the vulnerable areas of his body to end the fight quickly. I hit him in the belly with the flat of my blade. He doubled over and dropped his own sword. I struck his knees, and then slammed my weapon on his collarbone.

He stood and gripped his sword.

I shook my head. That beating should have taken him out for the rest of the fight.

He roared. His eyes flashed with a faint orange glow, and his skin cracked to reveal smoldering embers under his mortal shell. What was happening? I pressed my eyes shut and reopened them. Other than his irate countenance, he looked normal again. "I'm just losing my composure," I told myself. An unsettling feeling hit the pit of my stomach and goose bumps covered my skin.

My opponent tossed his sword at me like a spear. I dodged, but that was enough to draw my attention away from him.

I didn't even see him charge before he slammed me against the ground. My body hit the back of my armor and the world spun. He knelt over me, punched me across the face, and dislodged my helmet. With his strong legs, he pinned my arms to my sides.

I bent my knees and moved my hand to the dagger I carried in my boot. I grasped the handle of the blade. The arena filled with the sharp shrill of metal against metal as I scraped it against his armor. He stopped

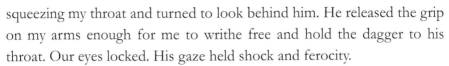

squeezing my throat and turned to look behind him. He released the grip on my arms enough for me to writhe free and hold the dagger to his throat. Our eyes locked. His gaze held shock and ferocity.

"That will be enough! Very good!" the captain yelled.

My competitor stood and backed away from me. I jumped to my feet and reluctantly lowered the dagger. I didn't trust him and, somehow, I felt this fight wasn't over.

The king clapped and shouted, "Bravo, bravo!"

I touched my lip. It was bleeding. I wiped my mouth so no one would see me bleed, especially when I had fought poorly. I could feel my competitor's eyes scrutinizing me. I cast a quick sideways glance at him. He stared at the blood on my lip with a ravaging hunger. I blinked. What a pervert. Or was it something else? Why was he looking at my blood like that?

He didn't take his eyes off me until the king asked both of us for our names.

My competitor said, "Lord Randal, from Tundis."

I had never heard of it before, and I knew my geography well. He was lying.

"I am Bronson," the dwarf's voice answered from my own mouth.

"Bronson, you are a well-trained tactician," the king complimented.

I started to curtsy, then stopped halfway and gave an awkward bow.

"I wish I could have a show like that every day."

It was kind of gross how the king thought this was a game. Someone could have died. I twisted my lips and forced a smile.

The captain continued, "There are three groups of thirty, which means each of you will fight again tomorrow before you are accepted into the guard. From there, you will serve your king and prove if you are

worthy of knighthood."

My teeth snapped together and I inwardly groaned. One more fight? I just wanted a good long soak in a warm tub.

The king dismissed us, and I retreated through the open gate. I kept my stride and tried not to limp like an injured lamb, at least not until I got into the hall. I couldn't believe I had gotten distracted and allowed him to pin me. That could've ended badly.

I limped to my barrack where Ruburt waited for me. My defeated comrades had already packed and left the castle. "At least I have my own room now," I scoffed in Ruburt's deep voice, though the price wasn't worth the luxury.

I pulled a glittering object out of my pack.

"The necklace!" Ruburt exclaimed in a silvery soprano tone. He coughed, and I chuckled at him in his own voice. We both looked at Cassi.

The pixie waved her wand over us. "Voices change back to where voices came."

The dwarf tested his voice once more, "Uh, hemm . . ." He shook his head and scolded, "Warn me before you do that again! You have no idea the uproar this pixie magic caused when I answered someone who asked me for directions to the armory!" Cassi snickered. Ruburt ignored her and turned to me. "I thought the necklace was still at the manor."

"Alwaien gave it back to me." I averted my gaze and hoped Ruburt wouldn't press for the details of that horrible night. "I am going to use it to heal these bruises from the duel. The captain wants me to fight again tomorrow. I think he's counting on the beating I took today to wear me down."

"That scoundrel!" Ruburt growled through his teeth. "That's the kind of low blow I'd expect from someone working for the Shadow Legion."

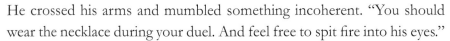

He crossed his arms and mumbled something incoherent. "You should wear the necklace during your duel. And feel free to spit fire into his eyes."

"Ruburt," I tried to sound serious, but the image of me actually spitting fire into the captain's eyes was so out of my character, it made me laugh. "Then everyone will know I'm a Neviahan."

I slipped the chain around my neck and fastened the clasp. I closed my eyes as a wave of hot wind seemed to flow through my body. I opened my eyes and watched my bruises and scrapes disappear. "It's working." My mind felt clearer. My memory of the fight became distinct and crisp. I recalled Lord Randal's eyes flashing like embers and his flesh starting to burst off his frame before he stopped himself from revealing what was underneath his skin. "This Lord Randal," I said out loud, "I've seen him before."

It became horribly clear. He was the same man who tried to convince my village that I was a witch when I was thirteen. I could barely get the words out, "He's a Shadow Lord."

"What?" Ruburt asked.

"It's him. I'm sure of it. That's why he was looking at my blood with hunger."

From the hall, chainmail clinked together and heavy boots pounded in a furious stride.

"Hide. Now," I whispered. My eyes darted around the room.

"There." Ruburt pointed to a pile of wood next to a fire-pit. We crouched low to the ground behind the messy pile of wood.

Randal burst into the room. His irate expression and burning gaze flashed like a firestorm in his eyes, drowning out all natural color. His round pupils focused and shrunk to a long slit like a snake's.

It was he who started this whole mess. He started the fires that killed

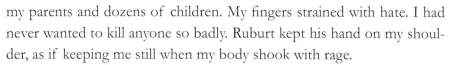

my parents and dozens of children. My fingers strained with hate. I had never wanted to kill anyone so badly. Ruburt kept his hand on my shoulder, as if keeping me still when my body shook with rage.

The captain of the guard ambled behind Randal casually. "I highly doubt his blood was Neviahan. You're just irritated because you didn't obliterate the only sober person in the competition. We tried to get them all drunk so they couldn't fight. I guess one slipped through." He looked at his fingernails nonchalantly and leaned against the doorframe. "Besides, if that warrior was a Neviahan, he would have killed you."

"I'm positive he was one," Randal said. "I could feel myself getting stronger as I imagined drinking his blood." His gazed stopped at the firewood where we hid. I peered through the cracks in the wood. Randal approached our hiding spot. His feet hit the ground like an executioner's drum. My muscles tightened as I reached for my dagger.

The captain grabbed Randal's tunic and spun him around. "I am the one who gets the Neviahan blood."

I met Ruburt's eyes. He looked like he was about to faint. He mouthed the words, "Shadow Lords."

The captain continued, "Surely, you understand that I have to do something to get Erebus's attention. Just think of what I could do with Neviahan power. When the time comes, you can take King Henry's body. Then we will both be powerful."

"Forget the king's human blood. I'm tired of human blood," Randal complained. "I want Neviahan blood. Maybe we can share the Neviahan's blood and the power."

"I get all the Neviahan blood and power," the captain argued. "The king's identity is not a bad trade—the Neviahan for the king. At least you will get to rule England."

Randal crossed his arms. He didn't look convinced. I had the feeling this was going to be a race between the Shadow Lords to see who would kill me first.

Chapter Twenty-Six

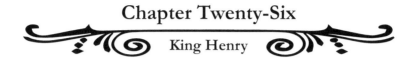

King Henry

I'd been through several lifetimes of changes—from an orphan, to a member of a noble family, a mercenary, and a knight in training.

But who was I? Was I really supposed to be the hero of this story? Could I, an absurdly awkward girl, fight the Shadow Legion and save the kingdom?

The sunlight beamed though the window and sparkled off my opal skin. The Shadow Lord had been right all along—I wasn't human. I was something much more powerful.

I had to warn King Henry about the two Shadow Lords. I stood to rush down the hall, but stopped. If I did, then the king would know I was an imposter pretending to be a man . . . and pretending to be human.

I turned to Ruburt and Cassi and said, "There is only one way I can approach the king without risking a death sentence." I pulled off the hood of my cloak and continued, "I must tell him who I really am–the Lady of Neviah.

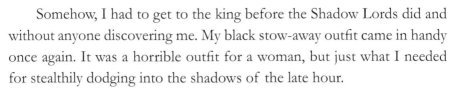

Somehow, I had to get to the king before the Shadow Lords did and without anyone discovering me. My black stow-away outfit came in handy once again. It was a horrible outfit for a woman, but just what I needed for stealthily dodging into the shadows of the late hour.

I slinked through the castle toward the king's room. An ambience of the Shadow Legion's presence haunted the hallways. I couldn't believe they were actually in the heart of London. If the Shadow Lords were able to steal the king's identity, as they had been talking about doing, they could destroy the government and enslave all of England.

I peered down a long, red-carpeted hallway, lined with suits of empty armor. At the far end of the hall, a single torch flickered. Its speck of light marked the location of King Henry's chamber doors.

I slid along the wall behind the armor and watched for any sign of movement. It seemed like hours passed as I inched my back against the stone. My muscles ached from the slow, controlled movements.

A soldier's boots clicked against the floor. I crouched low to the ground behind the armor. The captain rounded the corner. Panic sprang from the pit of my stomach and my mouth went dry.

"Captain," a man called from behind and caught the captain's attention. "There's a Shadow Wolf waiting at the gates with a report."

My palms grew slick with perspiration and my heart raced. Shadow Wolf? This just couldn't get any worse. How was I supposed to save the king while fighting the Shadow Lords and a Shadow Wolf as well?

The captain rolled his eyes.

"He said it's urgent. Something about the Lady of Neviah."

"What?" The captain shouted and strode down the hallway at a quick pace.

I covered my mouth and waited until I couldn't hear the sound of

their footfalls. The words rang through my mind, "Lady of Neviah." Someone knew. This might be my last chance to warn the king before these dark rebels tried to kill him. I raced for the king's chambers, flung the door open and snapped it shut behind me. "That was close." I leaned against the door, catching my breath.

"My lady?"

I jumped and gripped the door handle behind me. King Henry sat at his library, wearing a fine scarlet night robe. He smiled past his long mustache and short, pointed beard.

"I am such a half-wit," I muttered to myself and wrapped the cloak around my black outfit. I brushed my hair back. I had pretended to be a man for so long that I probably looked terrible as a woman.

"What can I help you with, my lady?" He turned in his chair and faced me.

I swallowed hard before saying, "I have come to warn you. There are several members of the Shadow Legion in the castle."

He didn't look surprised. "What is your name?"

"Auriella." I wrung my hands together.

"How do you know there are rebels in the castle, Auriella?"

"I fought one of them today in the arena."

"You? But you are just a lass." The king narrowed his eyes and stood. I bit my lip. What if he didn't believe me? What if he thought I was a lunatic? I certainly was dressed like one. He stepped toward me with an expression of amusement and bewilderment. "Could you really be the next Divine Warrior?"

I did not move. Divine Warrior? What was he talking about?

He held up a candle to shine light on my face. He stroked his goatee and asked, "Your skin, does it glisten in the sunlight?" His question seemed

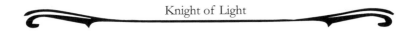

casual, but only someone who knew about Neviahans would ask it.

I repressed the urge to chew on my nails. "Yes," I answered in a small voice.

He sat back down and ran his fingers down the spine of a book with a worn leather cover. "Throughout history, the Neviahans have sent us Divine Protectors, but you're a . . . a . . . different."

I knew what he meant about me being different. I was a young woman and not a mighty man.

I brushed my arm. "I'm sure there is someone else, another Neviahan who is supposed to be the Divine Warrior. No one sent me, and I'm really not that powerful. I haven't even been trained yet."

"I see." King Henry smiled as if he knew something I did not. "If you haven't been trained, I'm sure you have lots of questions."

"I do, but how do you know so much about the Neviahans and the Shadow Legion?"

King Henry held up the book. "Only the kings and priests are allowed to own a copy of this ancient record."

I recognized the book. I had seen a copy of it on Woldor's shelf.

"This is the history of Neviah. I just finished reading about Lord Erebus." The candles in the room flickered. I held my breath as the name echoed off the stone walls. "Neviah sends warriors to protect mankind against the legionnaires." He gestured with his hand and offered me a seat next to him. "Maybe you can help me."

I took the seat next to him. "How can I help you?"

"I need someone I can trust." He gave me a sideways glance. "I think the Rebellion has infiltrated my war council. My council members have reported a decrease in the Shadow Legion's numbers, but more phenomenal events are happening."

"Your Majesty," I said too quickly. "I need to inform you that the captain of the guard is a Shadow Lord and so is at least one of the competitors. They plan to kill you and steal your image."

The king stopped smiling and pressed his lips into a tight line. "That is a bit of a problem."

"I'm so sorry about your captain." I sighed. "That's just one more person on their side."

"Don't be sorry, my lady. There is much to rejoice about. You, a Neviahan Warrior, are here to protect us. I know the druids haven't trained you yet, but I will try to answer all your questions."

I could only ask the one question weighing on my mind. "Are you angry with me for dressing as a man?"

King Henry laughed a hearty laugh. "No. Actually, I feel sorry for you. It cannot be easy for a beautiful young woman to act like a man." The king laughed again and shook his head. I did not know whether to laugh with him or not. "I will provide you with a room of your own, fit for a lady, with warm baths and fine bedding."

"Really?" I felt a smile spread across my face.

King Henry patted my hand and nodded. "Come with me."

Together we walked down the hallway to another wing of the castle. I kept a wary eye out for the captain, the Shadow Wolves, and other Shadow Lords.

The king opened a door to a large room. The first thing I noticed was the tall bed and a spacious balcony that would have a splendid view of the sunrises. Ivory linen accented by black velvet cascaded down the bedpost and balcony doors.

"A friend of mine is acting as my squire. Where will he stay?" I asked.

"Right next to your room," the king answered. "I will send for him, and your belongings, immediately. After your fight tomorrow, I will announce that you will be on the council to help exterminate the rebels."

King Henry stopped. A smile turned on his lips. "That is, if you still want to fight tomorrow."

"Oh, yes, I want to fight the Shadow Legion more than anything. Now that I know what I'm fighting, I will be better prepared."

King Henry nodded and laughed as he rubbed his hands together. "Those traitorous rebels won't expect the thorns of a young rose to be my lethal protection."

Chapter Twenty-Seven

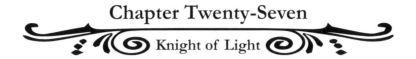 Knight of Light

I paced outside the arena. Any moment the herald would call my name, the name I had adopted as part of my false identity. The Shadow Lord I would face had killed my parents and almost killed me. This time, I knew my identity and power. A new fire filled me. I was not afraid. Maybe I'd even spit fire into Randal's eyes.

I tucked the ruby necklace under my armor and placed the helmet on my head. The helmet was the only metal armor we were allowed to wear for this fight. The rest of the armor was leather. The flexible armor allowed me to use my battlefield strengths—speed and agility.

The herald blew a horn and called for "Bronson" to enter the arena. The crowd cheered.

I met Randal in the center of the arena and stood across from him. His savage expression held the intensity of a wild dragon. His false human eyes shifted erratically.

"I know who you are," I muttered just loud enough for him to hear

above the cheering crowd. "Shadow Legion," I pronounced the name hatefully.

A flash of flames went through his snake-like eyes. "I remember who you are." Randal's words came out in a series of hisses. "The girl who couldn't be burned."

I nodded. "You were right. I'm not human, but I'm not a witch. I'm something much more powerful."

"Neviahan." His nostrils flared. "I look forward to drinking your blood."

"Begin!" King Henry commanded.

My dagger sped toward his ribs. He jumped back. I spun my sword around my head once and hit the top of his shoulder. He switched the sword to his left hand and jabbed at me. I flipped his sword into his face, hitting him under his eye.

He took a chance and blindly whirled his sword around. It smashed into my shoulder blade. I gasped and repressed a cry when I heard the bone snap. I think everyone in the arena heard my body break.

He yanked his sword from my wound. The ruby necklace worked quickly and heat replaced searing pain. I lunged forward and rammed my elbow into the Shadow Lord's ribs. He doubled over when my elbow found its mark.

"Go back to the darkness you came from," I spat.

Randal narrowed his eyes. His sharp tongue whipped out from his lips and cut into the side of my face. I stood tense, not even flinching, as a stream of fresh blood trickled down my cheek.

He tasted the sample of my blood. "You are the one Erebus has been looking for. You are Neviahan's secret weapon. Just one drop of your sweet blood can . . .." Fire burst from his hands. "Yes!" Randal crowed. "I

must have more of your power."

I grabbed him by his helmet, flipped him onto the ground, and thrust my sword through his ribs. His body convulsed as he cackled. Dark blood gurgled from the wound. His stolen mortal shell melted away. His laughter grew louder. A fiery being rose from the lifeless body and black flames billowed around the massive beast. He towered over me. His skin smoldered like molten lava over a muscular frame. Sulfuric eyes and breath fumed from his shadowy skull. The crowd screamed and raced for the exits. The Shadow Lord circled me, leaving a trail of burning brimstone behind him. He bent low and roared like a lethal jungle cat.

I stood my ground. He was trying to intimidate me, which meant only one thing, he was afraid. I gripped my sword. I couldn't let him have any more of my blood. Just one drop generated an enormous amount of energy.

Fire sprang from my hands and up my sword. The Legionnaire flung me against a stone wall with his massive claws. I gripped my burning sword and rebounded off the wall into the legionnaire.

I lunged through the inferno and sliced into the beast with my fiery sword. The monster screamed in agony. I landed in the sand on the other side of the arena and rolled from the force of momentum.

The legionnaire's molten skin crumbled like dried leaves in a furnace. A wall of fire billowed throughout the arena. I soaked in the heat, taming the inferno that erupted from the dying Shadow Lord.

A final blast exploded. I strained to contain the fireball rushing toward the bystanders and threatening to bring down the whole arena.

My hands sweltered from the intense heat. I struggled to gain control over the tempest of swirling fumes and flames. I dropped to my knees and pressed the massive firestorm into the sand on the arena floor. The

sand melted, creating a pool of bubbling, liquid glass.

I stayed on my knees in the charred arena, catching my breath as ashes floated down like hot, black snow. The ruby necklace chilled my skin. The foe was, indeed, no more. The crowd paused with astonishment before bursting into applause. I rose to my feet. My head whirled with vertigo, but I braced myself against my sword and bowed dutifully to King Henry.

I still hadn't taken my helmet off, but there was no denying my power and identity as Neviahan. Hundreds of people witnessed me create fire and defeat the Shadow Lord.

King Henry stood and raised his hands in the air, quieting the excited crowd. "A Divine Warrior from the Kingdom of Neviah has come to save us all!"

Men and women, peasants and nobles were on their feet yelling, "Hazzah!" Many of the women, and a few of the men, had tears in their eyes.

"That's my warrior!" someone shouted. I recognized the voice immediately. Philip and my brother mercenaries clanked their swords against their shields.

I placed my hand over my heart and whispered, "Thank you." I saw a tear-drop sparkle on the rim of Philip's eye before he wiped it away.

Ruburt sat on the front row with Philip. His beard glowed slightly and shimmered with pixie dust where Cassi liked to hide.

The king and several of his attendants entered the arena. I dropped to one knee and bowed my head when he approached.

"Auriella," the king said just loud enough for me to hear. "It's time to show the world who you are. Hand me your sword."

Butterflies took flight in my stomach. What if the kingdom

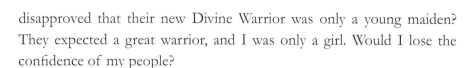

disapproved that their new Divine Warrior was only a young maiden? They expected a great warrior, and I was only a girl. Would I lose the confidence of my people?

"Don't be afraid," the king said. "Your heart is as strong as my best warriors and your courage is undeniable."

I handed my sword to King Henry, then lifted the heavy helmet off my head. My fiery hair spilled past my waist, and my satin white skin glowed with feminine youth.

Gasps reverberated throughout the arena. I noticed a few older noblemen scowl and mutter something unintelligible. Two young maidens beamed and sat a little taller. They looked at their mother to see if she approved. The woman shook her head, but her expression was undecided. Her two young daughters turned to me with admiration ignited in their eyes.

Sunlight broke through the clouds and flooded the arena, making the melted sand glint like a field of diamonds.

I looked down at my sparkling skin in the sunlight. I was different from everyone else, but I felt at peace. My power was a gift, not a curse. The rainbow ring shimmered on my hand, reminding me of what the fairy queen said. Just like a rainbow, I was from the skies, and my home on Earth was only temporary.

The wind caught the red and gold banners lining the arena and tossed them in a victory dance.

King Henry held out my sword and tapped my shoulders. "Holding the Power of Kings, I dub you 'Lady Auriella, the Knight of Light.'"

Chapter Twenty-Eight

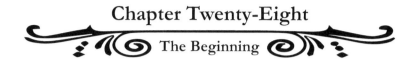

The Beginning

I lifted my indigo and silver gown and raced along the stone floor in jeweled slippers. I entered the moonlit courtyard where Ruburt and Cassi waited.

I noted the traveling supplies on Ruburt's pony. "Are you going somewhere?" I asked. "I thought you would stay for the celebration ball."

"I need to return to the dwarf village," Ruburt answered.

"What? You're leaving?" My heart sank. "Why?"

Ruburt came toward me and took my hand. "I have seen the Lady of Neviah with my own eyes. My people have been waiting centuries for you to come. It is time for me to rejoin my people and tell them you are here."

I bit my bottom lip to keep it from quivering.

Ruburt took a deep breath. "You are where you belong, and I need to return to the place I belong. You might not know it, but you have taught me much about courage and dreaming. When I return to my village, I'm going to fill my new life with the treasures that really matter." Ruburt

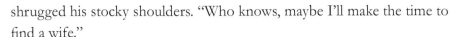

shrugged his stocky shoulders. "Who knows, maybe I'll make the time to find a wife."

I couldn't help but smile. Ruburt would make a fine husband.

Cassi sobbed and pulled at her dark hair. She fluttered to Ruburt and asked, "Ruburt miss Cassi?"

Ruburt slumped. "Yes, I'll miss you, Cassi."

"Cassi miss fish-eater Ruburt, too." She kissed the tip of his nose.

Ruburt's cheeks grew cherry red.

Cassi flew to me, then returned to Ruburt. She shook her head before flying back to me.

I saw Cassi's inner struggle and held out my hand for the pixie to sit on. "Cassi, you can stay here at the castle with me or return with Ruburt to the Golden Valley in the forest."

I would desperately miss them, but I didn't want to hold my friends back from living the lives they wanted to live.

Cassi fluttered around me then kissed me on the cheek.

Ruburt held his breath as the pixie flew to him. Both honor and horror appeared on his face. "Me? You want to stay with me?"

Cassi nodded.

Ruburt's grin turned into a frown. "Well, all right then," he tried to sound serious. "But we need to set some boundaries in our relationship."

Cassi flew into the air and danced with glee.

"Humph . . ." Ruburt mumbled, "Pixies."

We had been through so much and shared a bond three people of different origins rarely experience.

I held my hands to my heart. "Thank you. If it wasn't for you, I—"

Ruburt shook his head and stopped me. "You were always meant to do great things, whether or not we came into your life."

I smiled. "But only loyal friends would stand by my side against every odd to become a knight."

I pressed a smile onto my face and held back tears as I watched Ruburt mount his pony and ride from the courtyard with Cassi in his beard. I wrapped my arms around my waist and bowed my head.

"There you are," Philip called to me. "Are you intentionally avoiding the ball in your honor?" He took my hand. "You already have a line of young knights and lords waiting to claim dances with you."

I took a deep breath and looked down the dark road, then up at the lit castle. I had lived my life repressing my power and trying to be human instead of embracing my ethereal heritage. It was time to change all that.

There were still rebels to fight, a country to protect, and a war to win. It was time for me to start my new life as a Neviahan Knight of Light.

I smiled. "But only loyal friends would stand by my side against every odd to become a knight."

I pressed a smile onto my face and held back tears as I watched Ruburt mount his pony and ride from the courtyard with Cassi in his beard. I wrapped my arms around my waist and bowed my head.

"There you are," Philip called to me. "Are you intentionally avoiding the ball in your honor?" He took my hand. "You already have a line of young knights and lords waiting to claim dances with you."

I took a deep breath and looked down the dark road, then up at the lit castle. I had lived my life repressing my power and trying to be human instead of embracing my ethereal heritage. It was time to change all that.

There were still rebels to fight, a country to protect, and a war to win. It was time for me to start my new life as a Neviahan Knight of Light.

About the Author

Deirdra (pronounced: Dare-dra) is a professional speaker in various venues, including radio and television interviews, and nationally recognized writers conferences. Through her company, Eden Literary, she enjoys helping other authors reach their dreams.

She has spent the last decade captivating audiences of all ages with her novels and fairy tales. Her specialty is paranormal history and theology that delves into documented phenomenon and natural disasters of biblical proportions that entices indulgence of a fine line between fact and fantasy.

Deirdra enjoys jousting in arenas, planning invasions, singing Celtic songs, horseback riding through open meadows, swimming in the ocean, hiking up mountains, camping in cool shady woods, climbing trees barefoot, going on adventures with her family, and all forms of art, including martial arts.

Check out her websites at:

Books:
www.Knightess.com

Personal:
www.HerEden.com

Business:
www.EdenLiterary.com

Eden Literary

Sponsoring a book is all about opportunity. It is an opportunity for an author who would otherwise be unable to publish their book have a chance to fulfill their dream. It is also an opportunity for businesses and indviduals to support a worthy cause and obtain advertising in exchange.

Benefits of book sponsoring include:

Increased credibility
Highly targeted market audience
More positive than most print advertising
Less likely to become "junk mail" or garbage
Better chances of multiple readers seeing the ad
Build brand awareness and recognition
Distribute samples or special offers
No worry about printing and distributions

Please contact us at
bookmanager@edenliterary.com
for additional information on sponsoring
a book or book tour.

zion's studio
PHOTOGRAPHY

portrait | family | wedding

zionsstudio.com

Eden Literary

Achieving Publishing Dreams

We help authors, agents, and publishers
by providing affordable services
to prepare, publish, and promote a book and author.

Editing and Critiquing
Formatting
Book Covers
Illustrations
Web Design
Writing Coaching
Animation
App Programming
Promotional Material
Press Releases
Author Branding
Book Trailers and Commercials
Printing
Distribution
Tours
Marketing

www. EdenLiterary.com